NEW METHODS FOR DELIVERING HUMAN SERVICES

New Vistas in Counseling Series
*Series Editors—*Garry Walz and Libby Benjamin
In collaboration with **ERIC** *Counseling and Personnel Services Information Center*

Structured Groups for Facilitating Development: Acquiring Life Skills, Resolving Life Themes, and Making Life Transitions, Volume 1
Drum, D. J., Ph.D. and Knott, J. E., Ph.D.

New Methods for Delivering Human Services, Volume 2
Jones, G. B., Ph.D., Dayton, C., Ph.D. and Gelatt, H. B., Ph.D.

Systems Change Strategies in Educational Settings, Volume 3
Arends, R. I., Ph.D. and Arends, J. H., Ph.D.

Counseling Older Persons: Careers, Retirement, Dying, Volume 4
Sinick, D., Ph.D.

Parent Education and Elementary Counseling, Volume 5
Lamb, J. and Lamb, W., Ph.D.

Counseling in Correctional Environments, Volume 6
Bennett, L. A., Ph.D., Rosenbaum, T. S., Ph.D. and McCullough, W. R., Ph.D.

Transcultural Counseling: Needs, Programs and Techniques, Volume 7
Walz, G., Ph.D., Benjamin, L., Ph.D., et al.

Career Resource Centers, Volume 8
Meerbach, J., Ph.D.

Behavior Modification Handbook for Helping Professionals, Volume 9
Mehrabian, A., Ph.D.

New Methods for Delivering Human Services

G. Brian Jones
Charles Dayton
H. B. Gelatt

Vol. 2 in the New Vistas in Counseling Series
*Series Editors—*Garry Walz and Libby Benjamin

HUMAN SCIENCES PRESS
Formerly *BEHAVIORAL PUBLICATIONS INC.*
72 FIFTH AVENUE, NEW YORK, N.Y.   10011

Library of Congress Catalog Number 77-1746

ISBN: 0-87705-309-X

Copyright © 1977 by Human Sciences Press
72 Fifth Avenue, New York, New York 10011

Copyright is claimed until 1982. Thereafter, all portions of the work covered by this copyright will be in the public domain. This work was developed by the Educational Resources Information Center/Counseling and Personnel Services (ERIC/CAPS) under a contract with the National Institute of Education, Department of Health, Education, and Welfare. However, the content does not necessarily reflect the position or policy of that agency, and no United States Government endorsement of these materials should be inferred.

Printed in the United States of America
789 987654321

Library of Congress Cataloging in Publication Data

Jones, Glyn Brian, 1935–
    New Methods for Delivering Human Services

    (New vistas in counseling; v. 2)
    Bibliography:
    Includes index.
    1. Personnel service in education.   2. Student counselors, Training of.
3. Counseling.   I. Dayton, Charles, 1936–   joint author.   II. Gelatt,
H. B., joint author.   III. Title.   IV. Series. LB1027.5.J63   371.4
    77-1746 0-87705-309-X

FOREWORD

"Damn it, how does anybody expect us to do the job with the resources they give us!" might well be thought of as the counselor's lament. Understandably, many of us see more program support as the salvation for human services—bigger budgets, more counselors, better facilities. When confronted with the need to do something different, even better, the "if only . . ." phenomenon frequently comes into play. "If only we had better trained counselors . . ." "If only people understood what we can do . . ." "If only . . ." And on it goes. The "if only" enriches our fantasy lives but seldom changes anything.

One day when we were engaging in our own brand of "if only," we imaged what could be done to assist counselors and helping specialists to develop alternate ways of delivering human services, to adopt and use systematic planning/evaluation methods. "Is it possible," we asked, "to present a model for the delivery of human services that would incorporate advanced concepts of organizational development, program planning and evaluation, and the application of a systems approach? The thought excited us. The more we talked, the clearer became the vision of a practical, how-to-do-it, example-laden monograph that a counselor could take—any counselor, not some super-effective bionic counselor—and immediately put to use. Could it be done? We allowed that it could. Shortly, we were back to where we had been with another "if only"— if only we could discover the right authors.

That discovery proved easier than we had anticipated. Clearly, the people who were totally qualified to do the task were a group who were already doing it, and doing it with notable success. So, as fast as we could place a call, we had our authors—a team of experienced pro's from the American Institutes for Research whom we respected and had a great deal of confidence in: Brian Jones, H. B. Gelatt, and Charles Dayton. They didn't disappoint us. We have what we believe is a useful stimulus package—a first step in helping all of us to change our ways, to adopt and use new methods of planning, organizing, and delivering our services.

So what we have here is an alternative to the traditional way of doing things. For some it may be a radical departure; for others it may be only a variant on their present ways of working. Thoughtful, stimulating, and prodding, however, it should be for all of us.

May we prescribe? Please drink heartily! Take in large gulps. Let it swirl around. Imbibe as if the survival of human services depended upon your ability to digest it thoroughly—as well it might.

Garry P. Walz and Libby Benjamin
Director and Associate Director, ERIC/CAPS

CONTENTS

Forward   5

1. **The Need for More Systematic Program
   Planning and Evaluation**   9
2. **An Approach to Effective Program
   Planning and Evaluation**   22
3. **Developing Staff Skills for This Planning
   Planning–Evaluation Model and Process**   59
4. **Using Competency-Based Client
   Strategies and Materials**   98
5. **Summary and Conclusion**   128

References   132

This chapter delineates some of the basic problems confronting human services programs—limited budget, increasing demands for "results," and the lack of the necessary skills to identify and effectively address student needs. In response to these pressing problems, a plan for the improvement of guidance services is introduced.

Chapter 1

THE NEED FOR MORE SYSTEMATIC PROGRAM PLANNING AND EVALUATION

The work described in this document has been carried out at the American Institutes for Research, under support by the United States Office of Education, Department of Health, Education, and Welfare, under Part C of the Vocational Education Act of 1963. Points of view or opinions stated do not necessarily represent U.S.O.E. position or policy.

PROBLEMS IN HUMAN SERVICE PROGRAMS

Human services programs have reached a juncture in their development that is at one and the same time the most exciting and the most threatening they have ever faced. On the one hand, the problems are more basic and critical than ever before. Clients are increasingly facing an ever more complex world and looking to human services programs and personnel for the help they need. Taxpayers are watching their taxes rise and yet are seeing educational decision-makers floundering for direction. As a result, they wonder aloud about just what they are getting for their money. Administrators are caught between these overtaxed, often hostile citizens, and staff members demanding even more money for the very services that so often fail to satisfy the needs. Human services personnel themselves feel caught in the crunch as criticism descends upon them from all directions and they find themselves unable to justify their role in the terms increasingly demanded. And yet, with all of these pressures, human services programs seem on the crest of a golden age. The critical need for assistance to clients in the areas traditionally covered by such programs is widely apparent. The expansion of responsibilities into new areas increases the possibility of providing truly enlightened, meaningful learning experiences for clients. New and imaginative programs and materials are blossoming on all sides—resources to do the job so desperately needed. In short, the potential is unlimited, if the problems can be solved.

Zeroing in on the crux of concerns, sifting the bogus issues from the real, identifying the exact factors to be isolated and dealt with first, is no easy job. But certain problems do stand out.

One problem that underlies not only human services concerns but those of educational and social institutions in general is the increasing budget strains that have developed in recent years. For whatever reasons, administrators are being forced to cut budgets. In school settings, for example, high on most priority lists for such cutbacks are guidance and counseling programs. This is largely because "counseling" somehow does not have a clear end product, or seem particularly important, at least compared with teaching English or science, for example. How can an administrator justify spending a sizeable proportion of her or his budget on guidance and counseling when s/he is having trouble paying for basic instruction?

What this comes down to, and what seems to be at the heart of the problem today, is accountability. How can those working in human services justify what they do, how they spend their time, where they allocate their resources?

How can they provide administrators and citizens with evidence of their worth, demonstrate to them in meaningful and dramatic terms the invaluable benefits of their human services program? Counselors have not done very well in this area in the past, partly because counselor educators have not taught them these skills. Candidates are steeped in the latest theories of behavior and counseling techniques, but left to their own devices when it comes to justifying their role.

Take, for example, a scene occurring frequently around the country in school settings today. This involves the principal sitting down with the director of guidance in the spring of the year to discuss the next year's funding. The discussions are usually quite frank: the principal asks in very straightforward terms how s/he can justify the guidance budget for the next year, given the shortages that exist. The response, when any is forthcoming at all, usually involves a recitation of all the innumerable tasks a counselor performs in a given day, from meeting with parents, to handling truancy problems, to referring students to other agencies, to counseling students individually, to changing registration cards, ad infinitum. The weakness of this answer is that while it tells the principal what counselors are busy at, it does not specify what they accomplish. How many students are different in what ways because of counseling? Answers to questions like this might make an impression, but few counselors know how to provide them.

A fundamental problem is reflected in the above description of the typical counselor's day. Going from task to task, responding to the greatest pressure of any given moment, the counselor ends up like a ping-pong ball. S/he goes from one crisis to the next, frantically trying to put out fires, with no time to sit down and consider the purpose of all the activity called crisis counseling, and it results in what might be called the survival syndrome for the counselor. The struggle is simply to keep one's head above water, to stay ahead of the next crisis. The problem with this approach is that it results in a human services program that constantly reacts to those who have reached the crisis stage, rather than acts to prevent such problems in the first place. The alternative is a program that depends on an organized plan of what each student should be receiving from the program as s/he progresses through school. Such a program, while it cannot entirely eliminate crises, can help to prevent them, and at the same time can reach out to all students, providing help to those ready and able to grow.

Such preventive and developmental programs can respond to another major problem: the growing demand to prepare students for the real world upon leaving school. In the past, guidance programs often coasted along by keeping a shelf of college catalogs and having a representative from the local smelting plant drop by in the spring for a talk. With the career education movement, sustained high unemployment—even in professional fields—and a growing student sophistication about school and the world of work, this approach will no longer suffice. Students want to know what is going to happen to them when they leave school, what their opportunities will be. And they want to know how what they are learning in school relates to this approaching reality. Fulfilling this need for career development is another of the challenges facing guidance programs today.

This is not a complete summary of the problems of human services programs, but it includes many of the key ones. Funding shortages, lack of accountability, crisis orientation, and lack of career development are unhappy themes that pervade the majority of programs today. If people working in this field could solve these problems, they would go a long way toward promoting general health and even buoyancy in the profession. Unfortunately, this is not presently happening. And it is not happening for certain identifiable reasons. One of these is the "counselors counsel" syndrome.

This term refers to the widespread feeling among human services personnel that they were trained to counsel, this is what they are good at, this is what they enjoy, and this is damned well what they are going to do. It matters little whether there are seven other activities that will effect the same or better results in less time for more clients. Providing instruction to large groups; employing and training peer counselors; referring clients to community agencies; supplying books and films in areas of general interest and need; organizing the program so that other staff members and paraprofessionals can perform certain functions— all these may be far more effective in helping large numbers of clients. But they do not provide the same kind of personal reward—that look of appreciation or those grateful words from the one in need for the crisis resolved. Human services staff are well rewarded for individual counseling, in very meaningful, personal terms. But when this.activity dominates their schedules, can they legitimately claim that they are helping the most clients in the most effective way possible?

The reason for this syndrome, of course, stems partly from the education such persons receive. Individual counseling is usually what they are taught to do best. The same reason helps to explain their generally ineffective response to the call for accountability. They do not know how to be accountable. Faced with this situation, many in the profession react with defensiveness at best, out-and-out panic at worst. "Well, what we've done in the past has worked pretty well up to now. This new accountability fad will pass soon anyway, and we can get back in the old groove. Besides, aren't we doing anything right?" Unfortunately, things change, and the good old past is in many ways gone forever. Accountability is not a fad; many experts suggest that the trend is just beginning. And while the defensive "Aren't we doing anything right?" response is understandable, it will not solve the problems. Of course many things are being done well. But unless the activities that are not being done well can be improved upon, they may seriously impair the longevity of human services.

Thus, the funding crunch that educational and social agencies face, the crisis orientation of counselors, the "counselors counsel" syndrome, the lack of career development programs, the demand for accountability, and the lack of effective response to this demand, all add up to a serious situation. A solution is needed. If human services personnel could measure what they are doing; if, given this information, they could then plan a development program that did provide all clients with career guidance; if they could increase their effective activities and decrease their ineffective ones (individual counseling or otherwise); if they could demonstrate the results of their development program to those around them—especially those who have to make budget decisions—a solution might be at hand. But who can do this? Unfortunately, no one—at least, not very well; certainly not the typical staff member. Such skills simply are not a part of traditional staff education programs.

A POSSIBLE SOLUTION

Many ways to attack these problems and many possible solutions have been suggested, ranging from fuller use of technology to dramatic new human services techniques. One solution that is raising hopes draws on the research from a number of studies. For example, California recently surveyed its counselors to determine what were the greatest needs in the state, and concluded in *A Plan for the Improvement of Guidance Services in California:*

> Upgrading training for on-the-job guidance specialists is a necessity for improving present guidance services. The majority of those doing the job are now on the job and will be

for some years. Improving the pre-service training is important, but equally . . . important is the upgrading of those holding the guidance positions currently in the schools [The Guidance and Counseling Task Force, 1973, p. 39].

Similar conclusions were reached in a federally funded project conducted in 1972–73 by the American Institutes for Research (AIR). This study, supported by the United States Office of Education (USOE) and designed to determine the adequacy of guidance programs for those students not going to college, suggested:

> Comprehensive, well-planned programs of in-service education that focus on professional skills should be developed, and all school counselors should participate in them. These programs should help each counselor develop the skills s/he needs to meet revised certification requirements and to grow in competence so that s/he can advance professionally. These programs should be structured in close coordination with preservice counselor education programs that will result in concentrating on training in competencies to bring about student outcomes [Ganschow, Hamilton, Helliwell, Jones, & Tiedman, 1973, pp. 5–24 & 5–25].

Other studies have pointed in the same direction. And many of them reflect the stance suggested in the AIR study regarding the nature of the inservice education needed. This type of training goes under various rubrics, including performance-based, skills-based, competency-based, and so on. The key idea is that staff members need to develop actual skills useful in on-the-job situations. Traditional education programs have often relied on academic, cognitive outcomes, turning out human services personnel who may know a lot but are untested in terms of actual performance. While general agreement has not been reached on a precise definition for the term competency-based, it does seem clear that such programs should go beyond cognitive and attitudinal levels and require actual performances, either in simulated or real-life situations.

How can competency-based pre- and inservice staff development programs solve the problems discussed earlier? Ideally, such programs will show those in the human services field how to plan and evaluate their programs systematically so that they are responsive to the problems. A well-planned program can eliminate the survival syndrome and crisis orientation by requiring as the first step in the program development the mapping out of a set of goals based on measured client needs. It can provide a way to measure the program's effectiveness by translating these goals into behavioral objectives, with information collected periodically to determine whether these objectives have been achieved. It can counteract the "counselors counsel" syndrome by determining which methods and activities are effective and by motivating staff to spend their time accordingly. Because such a program operates from an overall plan of what all clients need, a key part of this plan can be devoted to their career development needs. Since such a program can determine what it does and does not accomplish, it can be accountable. Given precise information on what it is doing for clients, how they are different because of its activities, it can muster very clear, dramatic arguments for continued funding. In summary, a competency-based staff development program designed to provide human services personnel with the skills needed to plan and evaluate their programs effectively could ideally solve every one of the problems discussed.

Presenting the planning and evaluation approach developed by AIR (to be outlined and detailed here) as an answer to all of the above problems, however, is to misrepresent it. It does have clear advantages, no matter what the state of things—it was developed as a means of bringing fundamental improvement to human services programs regardless of the particular problems of the moment—but it is not a cure-all. One would have to be naive to expect to find the answer to every problem in any one approach. The following list summarizes, at least for school settings, some of the AIR approach's chief advantages and disadvantages, from a standpoint removed from the immediate problems such programs face.

Advantages of the AIR Approach

It is a way to:

1. Get counselors away from changing schedule cards, handling truancy problems, doing grounds duty, and the like, and into the important tasks for which they were educated.
2. Demonstrate to administrators, teachers, students, and parents just what guidance departments accomplish.
3. Zero in on what students need and want, and know that what is being done is important.
4. Monitor the quality of a program and make sure it is accomplishing what it is supposed to do.
5. Transform counselors from "people who like to rap" into effective changers of behavior.
6. Clean the cobwebs out of a program, eliminating practices everyone knows should have been stopped five years ago, seek newer and better ways of accomplishing ends.
7. Bring a department together under a common philosophy and agreed-upon goals.

Disadvantages of The AIR Approach

It is disadvantageous in that:

1. Staff members are likely to see it as a response to outside pressures for accountability which they resent and oppose.

2. It requires a great deal of hard work.
3. It involves the use of student behavioral objectives, which can be frustrating.
4. It may well reduce the amount of time counselors spend "counseling," an activity most are fond of.
5. It has a certain research feel, uses a systematic approach and terminology which may seem foreign, and will require a genuinely open mind and a willingness to try something new.
6. It requires change, which presupposes both an individual and institutional commitment to change, and an atmosphere free to allow change.
7. It offers no flashy new counseling techniques, simple cure-alls, or easy shortcuts. Primarily it is a way of organizing programs so that they can be effective, efficient, accountable, and responsive to students.

It should also be added that AIR has no exclusive patent on this approach. Operation Guidance, developed at Ohio State University under the direction of Robert Campbell and Harry Drier, parallels it very closely (Campbell, 1972). Part of their project includes the Career Planning Support System, a comprehensive approach for assisting high schools to upgrade their career guidance programs. It is currently being field tested in twelve states.

AIR has been working over the past 2 years to develop a system of competency-based staff development to provide practitioners with the skills needed to·carry out such an approach, and this venture may represent something of a breakthrough; but the concept itself has been expressed by numerous experts, and it would be unfair to represent it otherwise.

OVERVIEW OF REMAINING CHAPTERS

To summarize, we have now detailed some of the problems to which this approach can respond, and have delineated some of its strengths and weaknesses. What follows is a description of exactly what is involved in the approach (Chapter II), how the staff development program developed at AIR furthers the skills needed to implement it (Chapter III), and how some of the new client strategies and materials available on the market can be integrated into a program using the approach (Chapter IV). Chapter V provides a brief recap, and finally, there is a bibliography of books and materials related to the topics, or detailing materials available to be used with the approach. Chapters II–IV perhaps require a little further illumination.

Chapter II, "An Approach to Effective Program Planning and Evaluation," first overviews the entire planning and evaluation approach proposed here. It then concentrates on the first four parts of that approach.

1. Conducting desired outcomes assessments. This includes designing assessments, selecting samples, developing instruments, administering instruments, and summarizing and translating data into desired program outcomes.

2. Conducting current status assessments. Touched on here are summarizing program resources; analyzing current goals, efforts, and outcomes; and determining the current status of clients in the program.

3. Establishing program goals. This involves comparing the results of parts 1 and 2 to determine the discrepancies between the ideal and the current, drafting goals accordingly, and classifying and prioritizing goals.

4. Developing client performance objectives. An easy, straightforward means of establishing a set of program behavioral objectives is detailed, including both the drafting and sequencing of the objectives.

Each of the sections selects and summarizes one key activity from each of these parts and includes examples of instruments and/or products.

Chapter III, "Developing Staff Skills for This Planning-Evaluation Model and Process," details the staff development approach that has been developed. This chapter discusses the philosophical basis for the approach and some of the central definitions important to it; the focus of the approach itself; how it fits with the planning activities detailed in Chapter II, as well as with general human service skills; and then the nature of the staff development materials themselves, including: (a)intended target audiences; (b) example objectives of the approach; (c) format definitions; (d) sections of the materials; and (e) a discussion of tryouts to date. The chapter concludes with a discussion of some of the problems and issues involved in implementing this staff development approach, such as motivation of participants, sequencing the various tasks, coping with negative attitudes toward evaluation, finding ways of measuring improvement in participant skills, and making it appropriate for preservice as well as inservice settings.

Chapter IV, "Using Competency-Based Client Strategies and Materials," explains how client materials and programs can be integrated with the above planning-evaluation model and the staff development approach. It overviews current developments in client programs, and provides a synopsis of a number of promising ones now available. Details on each program include an overview, its basic goals and objectives, procedures and methodology, any evaluation information available, and a contact name and address. Programs touched on will include Human Development Services' *Life Career Development System;* the College Entrance Examination Board's *Decisions and Outcomes;* the Agency for Instructional Television's *Bread and Butterflies;* the University of Missouri's *Career Guidance, Counseling, and Placement Guide,* and *Career Education Methods and Processes;* the Federation of Rocky Mountain States' *Career Education and Satellite Technology Demonstration;*

the Baltimore Public Schools' *Baltimore Placement and Followup Program;* and the Cleveland Public Schools' *Job Development Program.*

The systematic model and process that the authors recommend for effective program planning and evaluation is introduced here. Following a brief presentation of the complete model, one fundamental segment of it is described in more detail. Activities that comprise this segment are summarized, and the tasks and products involved in one of its essential activities are reviewed in more detail and illustrated.

Chapter 2

AN APPROACH TO EFFECTIVE PROGRAM PLANNING AND EVALUATION

OVERVIEW OF THE COMPLETE PROCESS

As noted in Chapter 1, the program planning and evaluation approach on which we at AIR have been working over the recent years employs a systematic model that is based on scientific methodology and is aimed at the planning, development, implementation, evaluation, and revision of human services programs. It focuses on the needs and characteristics of children, youth, and adults. This learner-based orientation means that the approach assesses needs of learners and translates them into measurable objectives. It is upon these needs and objectives that priorities for human services interventions are based. Featuring a process in which each phase provides feedback to preceding phases or input to subsequent activities, this method assures that the genuine needs of your program recipients or consumers will be met in the order of their importance.

This systematic approach contrasts with typical programs, in which certain important phases (such as evaluation) are often omitted or others (such as implementation) are over-emphasized.

The model is goal oriented and designed to achieve clearly identified and, if possible, measurable objectives. The focus of the model is continuously on achievement of objectives. What is done, how it is done, and its success are all determined by these objectives. Feedback tells you, the program planners, whether to change your methods or to change your objectives.

In this approach to delivering human services, your program staff spends time seeking answers to the following questions:

1.   What do we accomplish?
2.   What do we not accomplish?
3.   What should we want to accomplish?
4.   What can we do to accomplish it?
5.   What is the best way for us to accomplish it?
6.   Did we?

For the purpose of simplifying communications, the model on which this program planning and evaluation approach is based is divided into four phases or groups of activities. We are reluctant to identify specific categories or to use the word "phases" because as soon as they are defined and even diagrammed in some type of linear order, it becomes too easy to think of them as having to occur in a lockstep, chronological sequence. This then distorts the whole dynamic and cybernetic nature of the interaction of those activities and their effects. Hoping that this warning is sufficient, we fall back on the easiest way we know to communicate this model in writing—a list, more detailed descriptions, and a diagram of the phases.

The phases are:

1. *Planning*: determining what you and your consumers want to accomplish and integrating this with system or institutional needs

2. *Developing*: identifying and putting together the best ways to accomplish what is desired

3. *Implementing*: putting your plan into action, trying out your selected activities

4. *Evaluating (Impact) and Deciding*: finding out how well it works and what to do next

The first phase, planning, is largely a data-gathering one. Many human services programs rely on insubstantial guesses and assumptions about what they should be doing. This phase systematically entails defining a philosophy, assessing the desired outcomes of your program consumers, determining where your program is at present, and then, based on these data, formulating needs statements and establishing a workable set of program goals. The program moves to a far firmer base, founded on comprehensive data and thorough analysis (see Chart 2.1).

Chart 2.1. Planning

Defining Human Development
Theory and Basic Assumptions

Assessing
Desired
Outcomes

Assessing Current
Status of:
a. Program resources
b. Allocation of resources
c. Current status of
   program consumers

Establishing Program Needs and Goals

Having completed the planning phase of your program improvement cycle, you will have established a comprehensive, practical set of goals, based on solid data and intelligent analysis. But these goals will be global, abstract statements which will fail to indicate exactly what your program consumers should be able to do. And they will say nothing about how you may expect the program to help learners to accomplish such specifics. The tasks of this second phase, program development, are also graphically illustrated here in Chart 2.2.

Chart 2.2.   Program Development

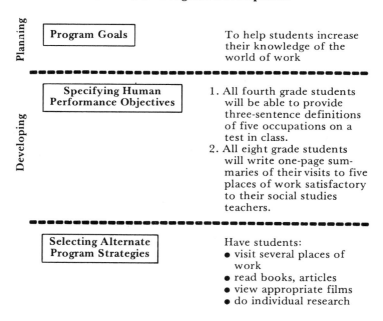

Planning

| Program Goals |

To help students increase their knowledge of the world of work

Developing

| Specifying Human Performance Objectives |

1. All fourth grade students will be able to provide three-sentence definitions of five occupations on a test in class.
2. All eight grade students will write one-page summaries of their visits to five places of work satisfactory to their social studies teachers.

| Selecting Alternate Program Strategies |

Have students:
• visit several places of work
• read books, articles
• view appropriate films
• do individual research

As the name suggests, the next phase, implementing, gets into the nuts and bolts of actually doing what you have been planning and developing. Each of the strategies will involve many individual tasks for the program staff and these may be thought about and planned in advance. The staff will probably be able to perform the vast majority of these, but you may have selected certain desirable strategies that will require further development of certain staff members. And as you go along, you will undoubtedly have to go through a fine-tuning process with new programs and strategies to work out the bugs and make them as effective as possible. Each of these topics is treated in this phase (see Chart 2.3).

Chart 2.3.   Implementing

In a sense, the fourth phase of this systematic approach brings you full circle. You began by gathering information to make intelligent planning and development decisions. Now you need to gather information on how well you have done. By doing this intelligently, you can then make further planning decisions and create a process of constant improvement (see Chart 2.4).

Chart 2.4.   Evaluating (Impact) and Deciding

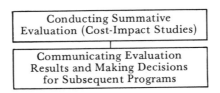

The above phases comprise the overall model and process on which we at AIR have been working. Figure 2.1

Figure 2.1. The Comprehensive Approach to Developing and Delivering Human Service Programs

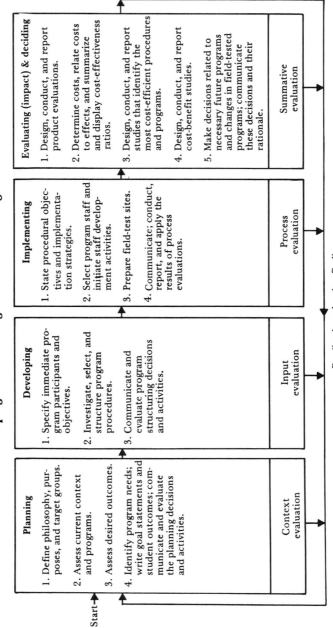

Planning

1. Define philosophy, purposes, and target groups.
2. Assess current context and programs.
3. Assess desired outcomes.
4. Identify program needs; write goal statements and student outcomes; communicate and evaluate the planning decisions and activities.

Context evaluation

Developing

1. Specify immediate program participants and objectives.
2. Investigate, select, and structure program procedures.
3. Communicate and evaluate program structuring decisions and activities.

Input evaluation

Implementing

1. State procedural objectives and implementation strategies.
2. Select program staff and initiate staff development activities.
3. Prepare field-test sites.
4. Communicate; conduct, report, and apply the results of process evaluations.

Process evaluation

Evaluating (impact) & deciding

1. Design, conduct, and report product evaluations.
2. Determine costs, relate costs to effects, and summarize and display cost-effectiveness ratios.
3. Design, conduct, and report studies that identify the most cost-efficient procedures and programs.
4. Design, conduct, and report cost-benefit studies.
5. Make decisions related to necessary future programs and changes in field-tested programs; communicate these decisions and their rationale.

Summative evaluation

Start

Feedback evaluation findings

27

illustrates the interaction of these four phases. The total model provides a way to develop and operate human services programs logically and systematically, which has been shown to be very helpful in many situations. But the system is not perfect, and it does not remove the need for hard work.

In order to understand and experiment with the planning-evaluation approach, you would need much more information than is provided in the brief descriptions and diagrams presented in the preceding section. A detailed review and illustration of all four phases of the model is not possible in this monograph. More feasible is coverage of one segment of the model, and the remainder of this chapter will attempt this. Discussed here will be the planning phase (except the important activites of defining human development theory and assumptions) and a key activity of the developing phase, specifying human performance objectives.

EXAMPLES OF DESIRED OUTCOMES ASSESSMENT ACTIVITIES AND PRODUCTS

Once a program's basic philosophy has been defined, the next logical move is to establish its goals and objectives. The key to such foundation building is identifying the important needs of that program's consumers. Human services are often structured around system needs. Needs assessments should give primary attention to the needs of the recipients of those services and should encourage the adaptation of services to people, rather than vice versa. They can also supply comprehensive data for determining the accountability of human services programs; give concrete, empirical data around which to develop programs; provide comprehensive data instead of isolated guesses; increase program coordination; and initiate a process of planning and evaluation designed to keep programs current.

To conduct such needs assessments requires asking program consumers, as well as other knowledgeable persons, to indicate their thoughts and feelings about what they need. A major part of the total needs assessment process is the assessment of desired outcomes. The process may be broken down into a number of activities:

1. Designing the assessment
2. Defining and selecting the persons to be sampled in the assessment
3. Selecting/developing the instrument(s)
4. Administering the instrument(s)
5. Summarizing and translating the data into desired outcomes

We have selected the third activity to discuss and illustrate below.

SELECTING/DEVELOPING THE DESIRED OUTCOMES ASSESSMENT INSTRUMENT(S)

Many different approaches to the development of instruments are possible. The most basic question is probably whether you want to use an already existing vehicle or develop your own. In either case, a varied assortment of approaches is possible. The following discussion presents a synopsis of the various kinds of instruments available for your use.

Kinds of Instruments

OBSERVATIONAL TECHNIQUES.   This method of collecting information involves watching behavior and tabulating data on what is seen. Usually such information is collected in real-life settings with the observer acting either as a participant (a group facilitator noticing group members' nonverbal responses during a group counseling session) or a nonparticipant (a child therapist using a one-way mirror).

INTERVIEWS.   The information gatherers sit down with the individuals from whom they wish to obtain information and ask them questions in a face-to-face setting. Usually they work from a predesigned form or set of questions to try to assure equal treatment of all interviewees. The face-to-face contact and personal touch are advantages of this approach, but it is usually time consuming and may contaminate data through personality variables that come into play between the two (or more) people.

QUESTIONNAIRES.   These are paper-and-pencil instruments to which individuals respond in any of a variety of ways. These include written responses to open-ended questions, checking "yes" or "no," checking one of several multiple-choice responses, ranking a series of statements from highest to lowest, and rating statements along a numerical or written scale. Questionnaires are widely used because of their efficiency and ease of administration.

FOLLOW-UP STUDIES.   These are surveys of individuals now removed from a program, such as graduates from high school who are asked for their thoughts on a high school career guidance program. A fairly short structured or open-ended questionnaire is frequently employed, but an interview format can be used. Mailing strategies often play an important role in this kind of survey, and achieving a high level of response is most important.

CARD-SORT TECHNIQUES.   This is a hybrid of the interview and questionnaire in which individuals can be given a

"deck" of cards, each with a statement relating to an outcome they might desire in a common area. Individuals sort through each deck they receive, eliminate those cards which do not represent desired outcomes for them, and arrange those that do in order from most to least important. When data on the desired outcomes of individuals are combined, the areas of highest choice and the highest choices within each area can be established.

THE CRITICAL INCIDENT TECHNIQUE.   Critical incidents result from the observation of identifiable behaviors that have a clear intent or purpose and at least one observable outcome. The incidents reported are of critical importance to the achievement of the outcome or to the lack of progress toward it. In one instance, critical incidents relating to ten abstract goals were collected from parents, teachers, and students, allowing precise behavioral definitions of the goals both in terms of student behaviors and teacher strategies to encourage such behaviors. A classification scheme was then built for each goal, and a series of "needs-assessment" questionnaires was developed to determine the extent to which appropriate student behaviors were being demonstrated. Thus, the critical incident technique served to define, in behavioral terms, the desired outcomes of the educational system. In another case, critical incidents were collected on counselor communication responses that were either effective or ineffective in facilitating client progress. These incidents were used to identify competencies, around which a counselor education program was later designed.

THE DELPHI TECHNIQUE.   This entails a series of intensive interrogations of samples of individuals (most frequently experts) by means of mailed questionnaires aimed at ranking desired outcomes and arriving at goals. The mailings are interspersed with controlled feedback to the participants. Responses to each mailing are summarized and returned to respondents anonymously. Competing opinions usually converge and diverse opinions are often blended into distinct and clearly stated majority and minority opinions.

Existing Instruments.

What often seems the easiest way out of the confusion of finding a good instrument is simply to adopt one that is generally available and thus make use of someone else's expertise. You are saved the work and expense of generating your own, and a ready-made instrument would seem to provide the simplest solution. Unfortunately, the solution is not that easy because a number of problems are involved.

The first difficulty is that in most cases such instruments have not undergone the kind of testing and refinement necessary to hone them into reliable, trustworthy vehicles for your purpose. A second problem is the fact that no matter how good the instrument, it will rarely lend itself perfectly to your particular setting—and will have limited generalizability since it was designed with the needs and conditions of a different locale in mind. A third problem is that few existing instruments make the distinction that we advocate between desired outcomes and current status. In an assessment, unless a program has information both on where it should ideally be and where it currently is, it is operating on very inadequate data. Most instruments just start asking questions, ignoring this distinction, and wind up with a potpourri of information that is of dubious value.

In mentioning some of the instruments already in existence, therefore, we also caution against blithely adopting them. Either adapting them or using them for ideas in generating your own instrument is usually a better course. Only those instruments seeking at least some desired outcomes information are listed below.

PRIORITY COUNSELING SURVEY. This multiple-choice questionnaire (Smith & Johnson, 1971) seeks a mixture of current status and desired outcomes information reported by students at various academic levels; separate forms are available for junior high, senior high, and college respondents.

MISSOURI STUDENT NEEDS SURVEY. This broad ranging instrument, with variations for students, teachers, parents, and employers, uses a multiple-choice format, seeking a mixture of current status, desired outcome, and evaluative information. It is available from the Missouri State Department of Education.

NORTH DAKOTA NEEDS ASSESSMENT MODEL. This six-point rating scale survey has variations for students, teachers, and administrators. It clearly separates students' responses into current status and desired outcomes categories, while seeking current status information from other groups. This survey is available from the North Dakota State Department of Education (Lee, 1973).

SANTA CLARA COUNTY EDUCATIONAL NEEDS SURVEY. This rating scale survey seeks students' feelings about where things are and where they should be, also trying to determine in what areas schools should help students. It is supplemented by a teacher assessment. This survey was developed by the Santa Clara Office of Education in San Jose, California.

Developing Your Own Instrument(s)

Because not all the techniques listed earlier can be dealt with in detail, we will concentrate here on questionnaires, as they seem to be the most generally practical. A number of questionnaire formats is possible. One is the open-ended written response, in which the respondents tell in their own words the answer to a question, structure their responses in the manner which is most meaningful to them, and offer individual insights. This format usually causes difficulty in summarizing the information, but does allow for individual expression. A second format asks respondents simply to agree or disagree with statements which express opinions on various aspects of the survey's subject. In a third kind, respondents are given multiple-choice items and asked to pick the ones that come closest to their view. A fourth format is that of ranking, in which various desired outcomes are listed and respondents are asked to put them in the order of their importance. A fifth format entails ratings, in which respondents express on a series of scales their feelings about the questionnaire's variables.

A number of guidelines should be kept in mind if you choose to develop a questionnaire. Begin by choosing the format that seems best for your purposes, and then write a sample set of items and have them evaluated to make sure they are appropriate and functional. To be useful as a guide to program improvement, each item should reflect a change in behavior, an attitude, or a level of knowledge. Items must be meaningful to the respondents. Language and wording should be appropriate to their age, grade level, or experience.

In addition, items should reflect the real needs of the respondents and not ignore important problems. Items should be ones to which they would be willing to respond, and should encourage response. Respondents should not feel threatened by the statements. Your directions should make it clear that there are no right or wrong answers, and your statements should reflect this orientation.

In addition to writing the actual items, you will need to draft some directions to go with them. Again, some general guidelines apply. First, the directions should be as brief and to the point as possible. They should explain the reason for the instrument and what it is to do. Be very concrete in this regard. If items on questionnaires are to be checked, say so; if circled, indicate that; if written out, indicate the length and form (sentence, phrase, list) of response you want. Often it is useful to include a sample item or two, with the correct form or response clearly demonstrated. If there are time limitations or other pertinent conditions which apply to administration of the instrument, be sure to mention these so that respondents can take them into account.

Once you have generated a number of items, you should pilot-test them. If you try them out on fellow staff members, you will often receive valuable suggestions for improvement. Along with this, and more important, the items should be tested with a few of your program counselors who are comparable to those to be included in the assessment. Suggested improvements should be gathered directly from these people and from observing how the process goes and what the results are. Suggested changes can then be made and the final instrument drafted.

EXAMPLES OF CURRENT STATUS ASSESSMENT ACTIVITIES AND PRODUCTS

Once the desired outcomes are defined, you will have determined the ideals toward which your human services program will work. But also important is knowing where you are at present. By comparing these two situations, you can determine just how far you have to go. Using these concepts, then, we define need as the difference between the current state (or status) and the desired state (desired outcomes).

A current status assessment involves gathering information through these kinds of activities:

1. Summarizing the resources available to your program. No matter how many desired outcomes have been defined, a realistic program must be designed—one that can be carried out with available resources.

2. Analyzing how these resources are presently being used. Since the most important resource is usually staff time, some measurement of how this is being expended is central.

3. Measuring how well program consumers can do presently in the areas on which their program will focus. These data can then be compared with their stated desired outcomes to show where the largest discrepancies exist.

Because the second activity is perhaps the most difficult of the above three, it has been selected for further discussion and illustration. In all of these activities it is important to note that a current status assessment is not designed to evaluate a human services program. You will not be determining whether a particular program is good or bad; you will merely find out what is happening.

Analyzing Current Allocation of Program Resources

One obvious way of determining current goals and efforts of a human services program is studying available documents. These will, of course, vary from one social action setting to another, but the following current documents are possibilities for study.

1. Statements of program objectives, desired outcomes. If the objectives have been documented for the program, they can serve as points of reference. As discussed above, a current status assessment is concerned with what the program is trying to achieve.

2. Program consumers' records. Records will not be the same for every setting, but such information could include

standardized test scores, referrals to counselors, interview reports, academic records, attendance patterns, and demographic information.

3. Follow-up studies. Studies of graduates and other former clients can provide information as to the respondents' perceptions of the program and how its activities have assisted or failed them.

4. Research or evaluation studies. If the program has recently undergone an accreditation or been the object of research, the resulting data may provide information that can be utilized.

5. Departmental budgets. These should provide all of the information you need to determine the allocation of your financial resources.

6. Community surveys. Studies may be available that show what occupations are most common in your area and what vocational and educational opportunities exist. Other studies may offer reports from local employment agencies regarding their perceptions of your program's graduates and their career or life preparation.

None of these six potential sources of information is going to supply the answers to questions regarding the current status of your program. Information must be gathered from a number of sources and analyzed as to its appropriateness and usefulness.

In addition to studying available documentation, another information-gathering method entails conducting time/task/cost analyses. Because in a current status assessment one of your concerns is the way resources are used, a time/task/cost analysis can be a useful approach. This analysis consists of noting the various tasks and activities performed by a program staff member, recording the amount of time spent on each one, and finally calculating the cost of each task on the basis of time spent. The record-keeping may be done by the person performing the tasks or by a trained observer. The results of the analysis indicate the tasks performed, the length of time they took, and the cost of each task.

For example, to determine the cost of an activity that required x hours of a counselor's time, this formula can be used:

$$\begin{array}{ccc} \textit{Cost of counselor's} & & \textit{Weekly salary} \\ \textit{time per hour} & = & \overline{\textit{Hours worked per week}} \end{array}$$

Suppose Counselor Davis gets an annual salary of $12,000 and works 40 weeks per year. Each week s/he works from 8:00 A.M. to 4:00 P.M. less half an hour for lunch and two 15-minute coffee breaks. For each hour of his or her time, the school district pays

$$\textit{Weekly salary} \quad = \quad \frac{\$12,000}{40} \quad = \quad \$300$$

$$\textit{Hours work/week} \; = \quad 35$$

$$\frac{\$300}{35} \quad = \quad \$8.57 \;\; \textit{Salary per hour}$$

Thus, if Counselor Davis is spending an average of 2 hours per day on clerical tasks, the cost to the school each day is approximately $17.

A time/task/cost analysis might also be made of other human resources in your human services program. However, your most difficult chore probably will be arriving at an accurate, reliable description of what your program staff actually does. A study in North Dakota attempted this. Counselors were first asked to estimate what percent of their time they spent in each of 13 activities (current status); then they were asked to rank the activities according to preference (desired program). A comparison between the two was made. The results are reported in the aforementioned *Needs Assessment Model for Guidance in North Dakota* (Lee, 1973). The North Dakota time analysis chart is one way to determine the allocation of staff time.

We have found that a daily log is a good way to record the activities, and it can be filled in either by a staff member or a trained observer. The log should be used for a 1- or 2-month period over your program's year. Ideally, of course, it should be used for the entire year. If the log cannot be maintained over a long period of time, it should at least be filled in at scattered intervals to minimize distortion.

The format of the log should not be so complicated that the staff members find it a burden to use. However, the form should include this information:

1. What happened?
2. Who was involved?
3. How long did it take?
4. Why was it done?

The answers to these questions can be brief, but each item is important. The first three are obvious parts of a log, but the fourth item—the purpose, or reason for the action—may not be. The question ties the staff person's activities to outcomes, the goal toward which the activity is directed; this is an essential part of the current status assessment.

Note this item from a counselor log:

> *Tuesday, March 14*
> *10:15–10:25, Visit by new student*

This entry answers questions 2 and 3, who was involved and how long it took—and gives a partial answer to question 1, what happened. It does not show, however, whether the student came in for assistance in enrolling, information about the school, aid in finding a part-time job, personal help in coping with a new situation, a get-acquainted chat, or some other reason. It is important for the human services personnel to note the purpose of their actions. Figures 2.2 and 2.3 are sample counselor logs that were developed in concert with the counseling staff of Cherry Creek High School in Cherry Creek, Colorado. They are offered only as examples and could be modified. For example, if you have formulated specific desired outcomes, the logs' sections on "Why did you do it?" outcomes could be replaced with your outcomes. By recording your activities in terms of the desired outcomes, you should obtain key data for a comparison of the current and desired status of your program.

In addition to studying current documents, conducting time/task/cost analyses, and collecting staff logs, you can add to your current status assessment by gaining information about the allocation of other resources. The current contributions of other staff members, clients, special personnel, and community members to your program should also be measured, as well as the current allocation of the many technical resources.

EXAMPLE ACTIVITIES AND PRODUCTS INVOLVED IN ESTABLISHING PROGRAM GOALS

This set of activities brings together the results of philosophy and desired outcomes definition and current status assessment in a set of goals that will serve as the cornerstone of your human services program. Program goals are the global statements of outcomes around which a program is structured. This set of activities also represents a juncture. On the one hand, you look back over the planning activities to make sure they have been of high quality. On the other, you look ahead to the more concrete definitions of behavioral objectives for your program consumers and program strategies to aid them in meeting those objectives.

Clock time (optional)

Instructions to Counselors: What happened? In the space below write down whatever information you need to jot down *at the time* to remind you of the other people involved and the purpose of each event that you participated in during the school day as a professional counselor.

Name _____
Date _____

(Use back of this sheet to complete today's log if you need more space.)

Who was involved? In the appropriate column below record the number of each type of people who were directly involved in each interaction.

- Students
- Parents
- Teachers
- Counselors
- Other staff
- Community representatives

How long did it take? Record how much of your time (in minutes) was consumed by each interaction in the column below that most nearly describes the type of activity involved in that interaction.

- Conference
- Phone call
- Decisions class
- Group guidance
- Staff meeting
- Desk work
- Seek & search
- Other type of activity

Why did you do it? Select the three most important purposes for each interaction and place a "1" under the most important purpose, a "2" under the second most important, and a "3" under the third most important purpose in the appropriate columns below.

- Orientation & enrollment
- Pregraduation planning
- Postgraduation planning
- Interpersonal counseling
- Intrapersonal counseling
- Decision making skill building
- Communication & coordination
- Program planning & evaluation
- Staff development & professional growth

Figure 2.2.   Cherry Creek High School Counselor Daily Log

Figure 2.3.   Cherry Creek High School Record of Counseling Outcomes

Counselor:_____

Date:_____

Number and type of contact

A. Student Outcomes on Which You
   Worked (directly or indirectly)

1. Orientation outcomes:
   Increasing knowledge of school resources
   Increasing knowledge of pupil services-related information
   Increasing ability to cope with the school system

2. Pregraduation planning outcomes:
   Increasing self-awareness as related to careers
   Gaining job-related high school experience and information
   Increasing positive attitudes and successful work

3. Intrapersonal counseling outcomes:
   Handling drug problems
   Value identification
   Increasing self-actualization
   Increasing self-awareness and emotional expression
   Developing self-confidence and self-love

4. Interpersonal counseling outcomes:
   Developing social confidence
   Building mutually satisfying friendships
   Increasing social awareness and acceptance
   Eliminating inhibiting characteristics
   Performing various social roles more effectively
   Acquiring more openness, sensitivity, and sharing

5. Decision class outcomes:
   Value clarification
   Learning the decision-making process
   Developing strategy and risk-taking techniques
   Developing a relationship between roles and lifestyles

6. Postgraduation planning outcomes:
   Improving career knowledge
   Gaining job-related experience and knowledge
   Gaining post-high school, pre-job knowledge and experience
   Increasing self-knowledge related to careers

7. Extra programs outcomes:
   Gaining experience in using social skills
   Developing interpersonal relationships

B. Other Outcomes and Activities
   (no specific student outcomes for these)

8. Clerical-administrative tasks:
   Communications regarding students
   Preparations for instruction and presentation
   Public relations and information giving
   Office and department administration
   Testing and evaluating

9. Meetings:
   Administration of counseling department activities
   Communication with other groups

10. Professional growth:
    Inservice education and training
    Establishing lines for professional communication

11. Other:
    Seek and search _____
    _____

Instructions: Please list the number and type of contacts in the top slot for each activity (see legend below).
Then record the amout of time (minutes) spent on each outcome category.

S = Conferring with a student   G = Conferring with a group of students
P = Conferring with parents   D = Conferring with a class
T = Conferring with teachers   B = Conferring with business community representatives
O = Conferring with pupil services staff   A = Working alone
C = Conferring with a combination of above

The activities in this set include:

1. Defining discrepancies between the desired outcomes assessment results and the current status assessment results
2. Specifying the resulting needs statement in order of their degree of importance
3. Classifying goals into useful overall schemes for a program
4. Setting priorities among the goals
5. Evaluating the planning activities you have conducted

Of the above activities, the third has been selected as the one to be discussed in more detail and to be illustrated.

Classifying Goals

You may wish simply to map out an unstructured list of goals, but more likely you will want to classify and group them. Grouping goals will highlight interrelationships among them, encourage comprehensive coverage of all important areas, make it easier to communicate them to others, aid in evaluating results growing out of them, provide new perspectives to those who use them, and clarify their meaning. The first place to look for such a classification scheme is to your assessment instruments. If you collected data in well-defined categories, you can simply proceed to determine your program goals using the same categories. Not all assessment instruments lend themselves to such easy breakdowns, however, or the breakdowns used may not be appropriate for a sensible grouping of goals. So if you need some classification scheme useful in mapping out your goals, the following are offered as suggestions that may be helpful.

One model developed at AIR divides the concept of "career" into six areas and allows all goals (and subsequent objectives) to be classified into one of the six career areas. Therefore, career or life planning and development is seen as occurring in each of these six areas:

1. Vocational. Behaviors related to exploring and making decisions concerning both opportunities in the world of work and personal characteristics related to such opportunities

2. Educational. Although often related to vocational behaviors, behaviors in this area involve exploring and pursuing educational opportunities independent of, or not immediately having, vocational concomitants

3. Personal-social. Intrapersonal competencies needed to function effectively as an independent person and interpersonal behaviors needed in small group situations, including two-person relationships

4. Academic-learning. Behaviors involved in handling difficult situations and varied learning tasks more effectively and efficiently in varied settings, not just in the formal classroom

5. Citizenship. Behaviors differentiated from those in the social behaviors area because they are appropriate to larger groups of people and to secondary (e.g., government) rather than primary (e.g., family) social systems

6. Leisure. Behaviors utilized in the exploration of leisure, cultural, and recreational pursuits; and behaviors involved in exploring one's personal characteristics related to such pursuits; making decisions on the basis of such information; and pursuing one's involvement in available opportunities

A second model, summarized in a monograph by the California Personnel and Guidance Association (1972), establishes three major categories of career guidance, and additional subcategories within them. Each category represents a broad area of learning content necessary to help students develop work, lifestyle, and leisure satisfactions and achieve desirable societal outcomes. The basic components and concepts identified in this monograph are as follows:

1.0 Career Planning and Decisionmaking
    1.1 Individuals differ in their interests, aptitudes, abilities, values, and attitudes.
    1.2 The understanding, acceptance, and development of self is a lifelong process and is constantly changed and influenced by life experiences.
    1.3 Environment and individual potential interact to influence career development.
    1.4 Individuals must be adaptable in a changing society.
    1.5 Career planning should be a privilege and responsibility of the individual.
2.0 Education, Work, and Leisure Alternatives
    2.1 Knowledge and skills in different subjects relate to performance in different work roles.
    2.2 There is a wide variety of occupations which may be classified in several ways.
    2.3 Societal expectations influence the nature and structure of work.
    2.4 There is a relationship between the commitment to education and work and the availability and utilization of leisure time.
    2.5 There are many training routes to job entry.
3.0 Lifestyles and Personal Satisfactions
    3.1 Work means different things to different people.
    3.2 Job satisfaction is dependent on harmonious relationships between worker and work environment.
    3.3 Job specialization creates interdependency.

Chart 2.5.   Strategies of Help for Human Services Programs

I
Direct Help
(Counseling with Clients)

II
Indirect Help
(Consulting with Parents and Teachers)

1. Individual sessions on:

   a. Drug abuse
   b. Peer conflict
   c. Family conflict
   d. Pregnancy
   e. Self-awareness

2. Group sessions on:
   a. Interpersonal relationships
   b. Sex
   c. Drugs
   d. Family problems
   e. Decisionmaking

1. Inservice sessions with teachers

2. Inservice sessions with parents

3. Parent/teacher conferences

4. Test interpretation

5. Occupational information

6. Educational information

7. Curriculum revision

III
Post-High School Preparation

IV
Administration/Coordination

1. Postsecondary education

2. Occupational information

3. Educational placement

4. Job placement

5. Test information

6. Decisionmaking

7. Values

1. Orientation

2. Records

3. Testing

4. Evaluation

5. Registration

6. Scheduling

7. Placement (educational and vocational)

A third and somewhat more traditionally oriented model classifies program goals partly according to the vehicle of help. This approach, adapted from several sources, identifies four major types of services a human services program may provide, and suggests possible subcategories within the areas. The deflection of the focus away from student outcomes and toward strategies of help is a weakness of this model (see Chart 2.5).

Other models exist, many of them useful and worthwhile. Your job is to select or develop one that best meets your own needs, and structures your goals in the way that will be most useful.

A part of classifying and grouping goals is specifying for what target populations each goal is appropriate. Inasmuch as goals are general and broad, they often will apply to an entire program's population. "To help clients to be more skillful in making decisions and solving problems" is an illustration of this. It applies to virtually any client. But not all goals are applicable quite this generally; part of the task will probably become developing a set of goals appropriate for different age groups. These may be divided simply into elementary and secondary levels; into primary, elementary, junior high, and high school; into youth, adult, and elderly; or broken down in some other way more useful to your setting. But some consideration of ages and target populations is needed when developing goals.

EXAMPLE ACTIVITIES AND PRODUCTS INVOLVED IN DEVELOPING CLIENT PERFORMANCE OBJECTIVES

Goals resulting from the preceding set of activities will be general and abstract. Objectives are narrower in scope and more specific. They are stated in a way that is measurable and quantifiable; therefore, they help you to determine if you are reaching your goals. Each behavior should also have a specific target group, should include the conditions under which it will be measured, and should have specific criteria defined for acceptable performance. The result of putting these parts together is a complete objective.

Activities that initiate the developing phase of this chapter's systematic planning-evaluation model entail tasks such as the following:

1.   Determining client outcomes
2.   Writing client performance objectives that include outcome statements and three other ingredients that specify the target group, the conditions in which the outcome will be performed, and the criteria that will be used to assess it
3.   Using available banks objectives
4.   Sequencing objectives according to the developmental skills of target populations and domains of behavior

Since the first activity is fundamental to the others, we have decided to focus on it for further discussion and illustration.

Determining Client Outcomes

Writing objectives requires you to think of performances of your program's clients which indicate that a goal has been reached. One of the first problems you will encounter in going from goals to objectives is deciding what types of performances you wish to include.

Many attempts have been made to classify human behavior and educational objectives. Benjamin Bloom (1956) and Krathwohl, Bloom, and Masia (1964) divide objectives into the "cognitive domain" (knowledge), the "affective domain" (attitudes and feelings), and the "psychomotor domain" (physical skills). Frank Wellman (1967) uses three domains (educational, vocational, and social) and three functional levels (perceptualization, conceptualization, and generalization) within each. The California State Department of Education, in its recent attempts to set forth a model, has renamed these functional levels "awareness," "accommodation" (internalization), and "action." Each of these suggests the progression from encountering and understanding, through internalizing and accepting, to acting on the basis of the knowledge and attitudes.

Figure 2.4 is a graphic illustration of the domains and levels defined in the California model. Chart 2.6 provides specific examples of the types of outcomes this model's proponents believe exemplify it. This model could serve as a useful framework for your outcomes (and subsequent activities) if you have not already developed a preference

Figure 2.4.   Three-Dimensional Model for Pupil Personnel Objectives

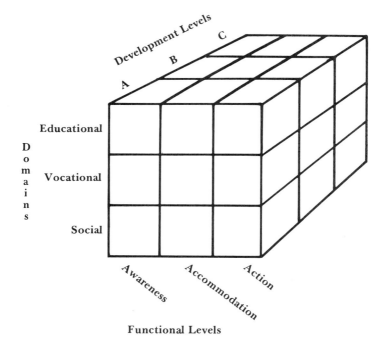

Functional Levels

Chart 2.6.   Area of Student Development Within Each Domain*

Educational Domain

Awareness: Awareness of the educational setting
                   Awareness of personal characteristics relevant
                   to the educational setting

Accommodation: Concept of self in the educational setting
                   Planning of work toward achievement of educa-
                   tional goals

Action: Coping with the demands of the educational envi-
                   ronment
                   Attainment of personal satisfaction from educa-
                   tional experiences
                   Achievement of success in pursuit of educational
                   goals

Vocational Domain

Awareness: Awareness of the world of work
                   Awareness of personal characteristics relevant to
                   the vocational domain

Accommodation: Concept of self in relation to the world to work
                   Planning of work toward achievement of occupa-
                   tional goals

Action: Implementation of vocational choices
                   Achievement of personal satisfaction from one's
                   vocation
                   Achievement of success in the pursuit of vocational
                   goals

Social Domain

Awareness: Awareness of social responsibilities, opportunities,
                   and expectations
                   Awareness of personal characteristics relevant to
                   the social setting

*Adapted from Wellman (1967).

Chart 2.6, continued

Accommodation: Concept of self in a social setting
Planning of efforts toward the achievement of satisfying and acceptable social relationships

Action: Coping with the demands of social groups with
which one is affiliated
Attainment of personal satisfaction from social experiences
Achievement of success in the pursuit of social
goals

for another scheme. The material is taken from the California Personnel and Guidance Association's Monograph 3, *Accountability in Pupil Personnel Services: A Process Guide for the Development of Objectives*, edited by Howard Sullivan and Robert O'Hare (1971).

If you are already familiar with any of these classification schemes or find one kind of terminology easier to use than another, act accordingly. But use some system. It will help in sorting objectives and understanding the interrelationships among them.

Guidelines for Writing Objectives

Certain general guidelines can aid in developing a set of objectives. A performance or outcome is a behavior that will indicate that the client has attained a goal. These outcomes must be related to the goal. They must be significant, that is, something you really want to know about this client. They must describe what the client will be able to do, not what others will do for the client. Outcomes should also describe the end result, not the procedures or activities the client will go through. They must be observable or measurable. Therefore, you have to use action verbs in your outcomes in order to avoid the pitfalls of vague, unmeasurable verbs such as "knowing," "realizing," or "understanding." These are difficult to observe and measure. Other verbs that produce ambiguity and therefore should be avoided in your outcome statements are:

know	fully appreciate
understand	grasp the significance of
really understand	enjoy
appreciate	believe
	have faith in

Action verbs are subject to fewer interpretations and are far more useful in describing what clients will be able to do. Action verbs that are useful in generating client outcomes are:

discriminate	give evidence	separate (group)
identify	apply (use)	design
recognize	make inferences	relate
sort	from	compare how
classify	choose (from a	contrast
match	list)	identify evidence
distinguish	identify	perform
compute	appropriate	list
calculate	interpret	draw
explain	operate	organize
discuss	define	demonstrate
state	record	predict (e.g.,
construct	describe	reactions)
make	write	name

Note how the action suggested by each of these verbs answers this question: What should a person be able to do to show that an objective has been reached? Such "acts" involve a performance that demonstrates a skill, a knowledge, a personal or social behavior, or an attitude.

As you think of outcomes, it is important to consider the developmental skills of the clients for whom the outcomes are appropriate. Behaviors that give evidence of attainment of a goal will vary with clients' learning experiences. If your program has a goal that is appropriate for all clients, then you will have to think of the outcomes appropriate for persons who have different developmental skills. These should not be determined strictly by age level, as individuals at a given age or grade level will vary in ability. They should build on one another, tracing a hierarchy from most basic to most advanced performance. It is at this point that subpopulations must be carefully considered. Individual needs and developmental skills vary a great deal, and objectives must be differentiated accordingly to be of real value. Think about what each client subgroup can realistically be expected to achieve. Match expectations to the real world. This is hard work, but essential for a practical, useful result.

An obvious question at this point is how many outcomes you should generate for each goal? The more precisely and completely the program goals can be spelled out in measurable objectives, the more likely it is that they will be successfully achieved. However, if for each goal you were to write outcomes for clients at each level of developmental skills for each domain, you would soon have thousands of outcomes and consequently thousands of objectives. This would be counterproductive to the purpose of writing performance objectives, which is to give some clear direction to your program. No pat formula exists for defining the exact number of outcomes and objectives for each goal, but clearly you must set some priorities among possible outcomes. We encourage you to think of as many outcomes as you can, remembering that not all goals have appropriate outcomes in all domains, or at more than one skill level. Then prioritize and select the outcomes around which you wish to develop complete objectives. To prioritize the outcomes, think of the criteria mentioned earlier:

1. Outcomes must be observable and unambiguous.
2. They must be relevant to the goal.
3. They must describe what a client, not a staff member, will be able to do.
4. They must be significant—something that is worth being able to do.

In selecting the outcomes around which you will build objectives, remember that the program should limit itself to those outcomes that it can reasonably and successfully manage. Try to select those outcomes that are appropriate to the program, clients, locale, personnel, and available resources. An important part of outcome writing is developing those that will best fit your particular situation. If this means having to choose a few from among many possibilities, the best course is to pick a representative sample that fairly and appropriately covers the ground in question. In actual numbers, a loose rule of thumb is to have from five to ten outcomes per goal. The best gauge is the considered judgment of the people working in the situation in which the outcomes will be used.

OTHER SETS OF ACTIVITIES IN THE PLANNING-EVALUATION PROCESS

We postulate that if you follow the segment of four sets of activities outlined above, the planning, development, implementation, and evaluation of your program will be facilitated. However, we encourage you to become familiar with subsequent segments of this process that flow from the results produced by the above activities. These additional sets of activities are briefly described below to illustrate the summaries presented at the beginning of this chapter.

Selecting Alternative Program Strategies

Knowing exactly what you want your program clients to be able to do still does not give you any plan for helping them actually do it. This set of activities moves from statements of ends to consideration of means. Now that you have defined in precise, behavioral terms the outcomes and objectives for your program, you need to think about how you can best help clients reach these objectives. Are the means you have used in the past the most effective? Efficient? Practical? Have you considered the myriad of other possibilities?

Specifying Process Objectives

Process objectives are analogous to client performance objectives in the sense that they spell out in precise behavioral terms a more general definition. But they are different in two ways. First, they apply to the program and what it must do rather than to the clients. Second, they spell out activities rather than terminal behaviors and therefore represent means rather than ends. When fully developed and organized, they form a plan of action that defines all the things your program must do to help its clients in the ways that you and they have decided are important. In addition, they define who is responsible for each task and the date by which it should be accomplished. In regard to assigning responsibility, they help you to match staff skills and interest with appropriate tasks, leading to what can well be a happier staff and greater program efficiency.

Developing Program Staff

In completing the two preceding sets of activities, you may have identified some areas in which it would be helpful for your program's staff to have more fully developed or additional skills. As staff members grow into their jobs, they can continue to seek education and develop talents that can make their performance ever more valuable. In this set of activities you explore how to go about locating and expanding such staff development potentialities.

Trying Out Activities and Monitoring Early Implementation Efforts

Evaluation may be thought of in two realms, formative and summative. The latter deals with program accomplishments and attainment of goals at something approaching an end point, looking back over a substantial period of time (say a year or more). Formative evaluation refers to all the feedback mechanisms used as a program progresses that detect and predict problems and help planners make ongoing decisions to make the program operate as effectively as possible. Exploring the ways to go about conducting effective formative evaluation includes deciding when it is and is not important to collect information, how you go about doing it, and how you make use of it when you get it.

Conducting Summative Evaluations (Cost-Impact Studies)

As the title suggests, two key kinds of information are sought in this type of program evaluation: the program's impact or what it has achieved, and how much it costs. Whereas in formative evaluation the focus is on the individual parts of a program, here the interest is on the entire program. Decisions are still oriented toward how best to improve the program; but hard choices about eliminating parts of it may be dictated by the results, and a longer-range view is required. This set of activities emphasizes how to design such evaluations and carry them out, and how to use the results in making important decisions.

Communicating Evaluation Results

If you have carried out the preceding activities successfully, you will have a well-designed and evaluated program. But no one may know about it—a situation that is more than a cosmetic concern. Other staff members, administrators, politicians, parents, and clients all play a vital role in decisions about human services programs. You can make effective use of your evaluation report with all of these groups. This set of activities entails three central concerns: decisions and the data they require, audience characteristics, and resources available for producing the report. It not only explores variations that can occur in the report content, format, and level of sophistication, but also investigates a variety of techniques that will improve any report.

SUMMARY

This chapter briefly reviewed a fundamental segment of a systematic planning-evaluation model and process. This segment entails conducting desired outcomes assessments, performing current status assessments, establishing program goals, and developing client performance objectives. It is our firm belief that this segment covers a critically important portion of the comprehensive model and process introduced at the beginning of the chapter.

These activities are invariably either ignored by program planners and developers or are quickly glossed over. The results are human services programs with ill-defined goals and "objectives," with an overemphasis on delivering services for these ambiguous purposes, and with an impossible design for any type of meaningful monitoring and evaluation. No wonder such a paucity of solid accountability evidence exists concerning the effectiveness and efficiency of many social action and educational programs.

A major problem in ensuring that such a systematic program planning-evaluation model and process is tried and tested is the lack of program staff skilled in its philosophy and techniques. There is need for comprehensive, well-planned approaches to inservice education that focus on the technical and professional skills necessary to implement such models. Such approaches should be structured in close coordination with preservice education of human services personnel, who are then able to develop competencies useful in producing identifiable, agreed-upon client outcomes.

It is to respond to this problem that inservice staff development is currently being developed and field tested at AIR. At the same time, plans are underway for articulating this educational effort with preservice activities. The aim of this staff development is to provide the deliverers of human services with skills necessary to effectively plan, develop, implement, and evaluate social action or educational programs. This approach is discussed further in Chapter 3.

Building on the systematic planning-evaluation model and process summarized in Chapter II, this chapter addresses the issue of helping human services personnel learn the knowledge and skills they need in order to employ that approach. The nature of one learning process is summarized and illustrated. General conclusions from recent pilot tests of this educational approach are stated, as are problems that accompany its implementation.

Chapter 3

DEVELOPING STAFF SKILLS FOR THIS PLANNING-EVALUATION MODEL AND PROCESS

ASSUMPTIONS BASIC TO THIS STAFF DEVELOPMENT APPROACH

Through the pilot and field tests of this and other staff development activities, we have painfully learned the importance of both making explicit the assumptions on which our design and implementation activities have been founded and stating these at the beginning of any presentation. In this way we do not take these assumptions for granted and our audience has an opportunity to review and challenge them, if they so desire. Such is the purpose of this section.

Assumption 1: The delivery of human services needs to be improved.

More specifically, we believe there is a need for more comprehensive systems of guidance, counseling, placement, and followthrough in a number of settings (e.g., schools, colleges, community service centers, correctional rehabilitation institutions, employment services). For school settings this need was well documented by an AIR study completed during the 1972–73 fiscal year for the United States Office of Education's Office of Planning, Budgeting, and Evaluation (USOE Contract #OEC–O–72–4986). After surveying the nation to find effective guidance, counseling, placement, and follow-up programs for non-college-bound youth, and producing an extensive literature review (over 150 pages), a final report, and 13 case studies, we concluded that programs had not yet been realized to meet the needs of such youth. Further, we speculated on the direction that should be taken by future attempts at improving such services.

> If guidance systems are to be realigned to meet genuine needs of youth as conceived by the authors, there is a major need for rigorous program development. The potential to conduct such development and evaluation requires explicit, clearly defined, and measurable program objectives and an accurate knowledge of the practical and political context in which judgments concerning achievement of these objectives must be made. Then data generated by a program must be: correlated with these objectives, as specifically related to the behavior of members of the target population; collected accurately; presented in an easily interpretable form; and provided in time to be used by decision-makers at all levels with a means to evaluate cost-benefits and cost-effectiveness [Ganschow et al., 1973, pp. 5–25].

The rigorous program improvement called for in the above statement implies the need for a systematic planning-evaluation process such as the one outlined in Chapter 2. *Assumption 2: Those human services that focus on influencing the career development of their clients should focus on a broad definition of "career," one that is more synonymous with "life."* Rather than define career simply as vocation, we view it more broadly as a life-development process which involves all the important elements in an individual's growth toward what s/he would like to be. The six elements that we include within this broad concept of career, listed and defined in Chapter 2, are vocational, educational, personal-social, academic-learning, citizenship, and leisure. In this context, career development entails many aspects of life besides those related to school and work decisionmaking.

Assumption 3: Many persons engaged in the delivery of human services presently lack the planning and evaluation competencies needed for effective program improvement, and should have competency-based staff development assistance. Staff development attempting to deliver the required competencies is therefore needed. We use the terms "competencies" and "skills" interchangeably. The staff development approach on which we have been working attempts to go well beyond the cognitive and attitudinal levels emphasized in many conventional instructional programs for human services personnel. We concentrate on the actual skills and behaviors such personnel require in order to develop and deliver comprehensive services. Such skills have to be operationalized by observable performances, preferably ones that can be evaluated by the successful production of a product having measurable relevance for practical settings.

Assumption 4: Insufficient information has been available for generating the type of competency-based staff development suggested above. Until recently no concentrated efforts had been made to implement activities outlined in the following process:

1.   Identify generic and situation-specific tasks that human services personnel perform in practical settings (i.e., conduct a task analysis).
2.   Specify competencies (initially stated as desired outcomes for such personnel) needed to perform these tasks (i.e., conduct a competency analysis).
3.   Select and design assessment strategies by which such competencies can be measured. What performance-based assessment techniques exist, what techniques are presently under development, and how can they best be adapted? Such techniques must assess the skills each partic-

ipant has, the one s/he needs to develop, and those s/he wants to acquire and practice (i.e., competency assessment).

4.   Design and evaluate performance-based instructional sequences (including materials and strategies) that provide learning experiences appropriate to the competencies selected.

5.   Determine how to evaluate the effectiveness of the staff development.

6.   Pilot-test, revise, and field test the staff development. Then, revise it again before integrating it into regular pre- and inservice training sessions.

7.   Validate the competencies produced by using experimental and quasi-experimental designs appropriate for determining the relationship between human services competencies acquired and client improvements made.

8.   Conduct data analyses to determine what staff development techniques are most suitable. What kinds of problems commonly arise, and how might they be avoided or corrected?

9.   Conduct evaluations by selecting appropriate criteria for assessing the success of the staff development series. Provide for the formative evaluation of the staff development used.

These are the areas to which we have been devoting our research and development energies over the last 3 years.

Assumption 5: There is a general need for more innovative and systematic educational procedures for developing human services staff.   For example, in the area of counselor development, several studies have suggested that counselor effectiveness may bear little relationship to traditional counselor education programs, both preservice and inservice (Joslin, 1965; Engelkes and Roberts, 1970). In fact, some counselors and counselor educators claim that the relationship is more negative than positive (Carkhuff, 1968; Island, 1972).

Cash (1972) challenged counselor educators to review their educational processes and to revise them, if necessary, to focus on program output. Counselor educators have been encouraged to specify in operational terms their instructional objectives and performance criteria. "Without specifically formulated behavioral goals, the accountability of a counseling curriculum is highly suspect [Horan, 1972, p. 163]."

New ways of learning and teaching are urgently needed in pre- and inservice counselor education; this is our fifth assumption. Counselor educators have been criticized for not making greater use of innovative programs and designs from new educational technology such as instructional objectives and modular packaging (Horan, 1972; Brammer and Springer, 1971). While the professional literature in education and in guidance has been highly supportive of the development of learning objectives and implementation of competency-based programs, few operating programs are in existence. Of those counselor education programs that have developed a comprehensive series of learning objectives, few have used modular packaging as a delivery system for educating counselors to use this type of information. We committed ourselves to developing a staff development approach that is relevant to all human services personnel, not just counselors, and is: (a) systematically planned and organized; (b) individualized and personalized to learners' needs and characteristics; (c) objectives based; (d) built around coordinated instructional modules/kits; and (e) sequentially organized on a continuum of increasing complexity of learning outcomes.

Assumption 6: There should be articulation of transportable staff development across pre- and inservice settings. The discontinuities between pre and inservice learning experiences have become more apparent in recent years. Competency-based learning can remove some of these discontinuities if it is tailored to skills that practitioners require in order to perform their job tasks better. As noted above, conventional staff development has not concentrated on the specification of job activities, competencies requisite to them, and instructional procedures designed to promote such skills. If these information needs are resolved, pre- and inservice learning experiences can be coordinated by an agreed-upon set of competencies, expressed as measurable objectives. To maintain its usefulness, such staff development must not only be applicable to pre- and inservice settings, it must also be structured so it can be administered in places other than where it was developed and by persons other than the developers. Perhaps at least 75% of each learning component should be transportable.

Assumption 7: There must be both individual and institutional commitment if human services are going to be improved. In many ways, this final assumption emphasizes factors that are well beyond the control of a staff development approach. However, human services personnel should learn to recognize the importance of these factors and have at least some preliminary skills for dealing with them. These factors involve system or institutional constraints that inhibit program improvement. Institutional openness to change and willingness to allocate resources that will facilitate program modifications are difficult to ensure. When it comes to challenging entrenched authority or ingrained behavior, many reforms go aglimmering. The influence of such attitudes cannot be ignored; these factors must be identified and, if possible, dealt with as early as possible in the program improvement cycle.

FOCUS OF THIS STAFF DEVELOPMENT APPROACH

As stated in the preceding section and in Chapter II, the staff development approach that we have been developing and researching focuses on the competencies human services personnel exercise in order to plan, develop, implement, and evaluate their programs. Chart 3.1 presents a condensed version of the knowledge outcomes and skills that we initially identified as particularly conducive to implementing all segments of the systematic program planning-evaluation model and process described in Chapter II. Notice that within the implementing phase, general counseling skills needed for individual and group counseling are included.

That domain of competencies is followed by Figure 3.1, which diagrammatically summarizes the preliminary set of modules that we have selected to provide staff development in high priority skill areas of the planning-evaluation model. There are 12 modules, the length of each averaging about 6 hours, or the equivalent of a 1-day workshop. Thus, this approach can take anywhere from 1 to 2 1/2 weeks. A coordinator is required to lead discussions, provide feedback on activities, and evaluate participants' responses to test items. A written guide is provided to help coordinators implement these tasks. More specific details on the nature of all parts of these module packages is provided in the next section.

Chart 3.1 Domain of Competencies

Orientation of a Comprehensive Approach to Program Improvement

Explain to another person the comprehensive approach to program improvement.

Explain the advantages of the comprehensive approach.

Explain how competency-based learning in this series is related to using the approach.

Indicate what competency-based learning, if any, is relevant to self.

Phase I: Planning Programs

Defining Philosophy, Purposes, and Target Groups
Define the philosophy and purposes and designate the general target population(s) of each program being planned.

Assess the current philosophy related to human services, and the current planning approach used; and, if necessary, work to develop an environment conducive to the implementation of the comprehensive approach.

Develop an approved, written statement of the philosophy and purposes for which each program will be designed.

Develop an approved, written description of each program's target population(s).

Assessing Current Context and Programs

Design, conduct, and report an assessment of the current context in which each program will operate.

Develop an approved, written summary of all assessment data collected on the general characteristics of the context in which each program will operate and the current status of learner-related outcomes related to both system needs and society needs.

Develop an approved, written summary of all assessment data collected on human services currently available in the target area. Such data should include statements of current services provided, outcomes those services try to help program recipients achieve, and the number of persons served.

Assessing Desired Outcomes

Design, conduct, and report an assessment of desired outcomes for program consumers in the target area.

Identifying Needs; Writing Goal Statements and Outcomes; Communicating and Evaluating Planning Decisions and Activities

Integrate data on current and desired programs in order to develop an approved, written statement on high- and low-ranking needs and wants of program recipients in the target area based on learner needs, and school system and society needs derived from empirical data.

Produce an approved written summary of sequenced goal statements and student performance outcomes for each proposed human services program.

Identify all audiences that should receive communications at various states of program improvement, their communication needs, media appropriate to their characteristics and needs, and a dissemination schedule.

Evaluate and report (in the appropriate dissemination documents selected above) the effectiveness, efficiency, and desirability of decisions and activities conducted during this phase of program design.

Phase II: Developing Programs

Specifying Immediate Program Participants and Objectives

Select each program's participants and specify program objectives related to the current status of each participant's skills.

Produce an approved, written description of the general characteristics of persons from each program's target population(s) who will receive that program.

Develop an approved, written set of objectives (including specification of the target persons; directly or indirectly measurable desired outcomes; conditions for testing, training, and/or real-life performance; and standards of performance) for each proposed program planned for immediate implementation. (Program objectives probably will reflect different developmental orientations at the various learning ability levels of program participants but should be smoothly articulated across these levels.)

Design, conduct, and report criterion-referenced assessment of the current status of each program participant's skills to determine her/his placement in the program.

Investigating, Selecting, and Developing Program Procedures

Identify alternative procedures for helping learners achieve appropriate objectives, and select and develop procedures for each program.

List all available and possible strategies and procedures that can be used to help participants achieve objectives which are relevant to their needs in each proposed program.

Produce an approved, written description of selected procedures for helping participants achieve each proposed program's objectives.

Communicating and Evaluating Program Structuring Decisions and Activities

Disseminate appropriate communications summarizing products, progress, and problems resulting from the decisions and activities of this phase of program development.

Produce for each communication audience, dissemination products summarizing each program's desired outcomes, objectives, participants, resources, and procedures in order to elicit ideas and support for subsequent field tests.

Evaluate and report (in the above dissemination media) the effectiveness, efficiency, and desirability of decisions and activities conducted during this phase of program development.

Phase III: Implementing Programs
Stating Procedural Objectives and Implementation Strategies

State procedural objectives and implementation strategies for each program and obtain clearance for the field-test evaluation, schedule, and costs.

Develop an approved, written description of the tasks which must be performed to implement smoothly and effectively the proposed field test(s) of each human services program. The description should list: (1) general tasks (*written as process objectives*) that program implementers should accomplish to ensure that participants in the field-test sites have opportunities to meet their performance objectives; (2) more detailed tasks briefly outlined as *implementation strategies;* and (3) *learner process objectives* that describe activities participants will perform to achieve performance objectives in their programs of studies.

Design, pilot test, and revise a support system (computer free, computer assisted, or computer monitored) to handle data on participant's characteristics and performance.

Produce an approved, written description of field-test costs and a rationale that describes the evaluation design, procedures, and schedule, and lists instrument specifications for assessing the extent to which participants in the field-test site(s) achieve their goals and objectives.

Selecting Program Staff and Initiating Staff Development Activities

Identify, recruit, develop, monitor, and evaluate professional and paraprofessional personnel who can implement the proposed field test(s).

Design and conduct analyses of the tasks that must be performed to implement successfully each program in the field-test site(s), and analyses of the competencies needed to perform these tasks.

Identify those tasks that can be performed by humans and those that machines can best provide, and then design and implement procedures for assessing the qualifications of available human and machine resources.

Select human and machine alternatives capable of supplying the needed competencies and identify options that need further development in order to attain satisfactory task performance.

Develop and test the desired machine resources as well as collect, create, and pilot-test competency-based staff development packages and train those personnel who do not have the competencies they will need. Training could be provided in many competency areas. For example, staff members should:

1. Relate effectively (language, rapport, respect, fairness, support) to learners, parents, and other program personnel.

2. Utilize: existing instructional packages or units; tests; various counseling approaches (e.g., client centered, existential, gestalt, psychoanalytic, rational-emotive, transactional analysis, and parent-teacher effectiveness); specific strategies (e.g., use a problem-solving process to help clients meet their needs; help clients acquire and apply decision skills; demonstrate personal-social contracting techniques; engage clients in role-playing and behavioral rehearsal activities; assist clients in self-assessment processes; help clients acquire and apply behavior observation and analysis procedures; help clients learn and practice self-confrontation; train clients in relaxation and desensitization techniques; employ rewards, punishment, and extinction principles with clients and self; and assist clients to acquire and use self-management and self-control skills); and explore various techniques for group counseling and guidance.

3. Analyze key factors of the institution (learning environment, relationship to the community, resources, requirements, strengths, and weaknesses) and their relationships to human services programs.

4. Be sensitive to contemporary problems (drug, racial, sexual) and traditional problems (family, academic, social skills).

5. Design and implement a staff and machine monitoring, evaluation, and renewal process to ensure that implementation tasks are performed effectively.

Preparing Field-Test Sites

Prepare the field-test site(s) and conduct and report process evaluations of implementation activities.

Prepare site(s) that are equipped with the materials and resources needed to implement each program in the field test(s).

Implement each field-test program as described in its process objectives and analyze positive and negative side effects.

Conducting, Communicating, and Applying Results from Process Evaluations

Design and conduct ongoing process evaluations of the effectiveness, efficiency, and desirability of program implementation decisions and activities; report the results of these evaluations to appropriate audiences; and make decisions related to subsequent program implementation based upon them.

*Phase IV: Making Decisions Based
on Program Costs and Impact*

Conducting and Reporting Summative Evaluations

Design, conduct, and report product evaluations to assess the impact of each human services program implemented in the field site(s).

Determine if participants have satisfied their needs after they have participated in the field-test program(s).

Determine if the satisfaction of participants' needs can be attributed to the effects of the field-test program(s).

Determine any unanticipated effects (positive and negative) of the field-test program(s) on participants, staff, parents, and the field-test settings.

Determine the cost of the field-test program(s), relate these costs to the effects of such program(s), and summarize and display cost-effectiveness ratios using both types of data.

Conducting and Reporting Cost-Efficiency Evaluations

Design, conduct, and report quasi-experimental or true experimental studies that identify the most cost-efficient procedures and programs for helping learners achieve their career planning and development objectives.

Conducting and Reporting Cost-Benefit Evaluations

Design, conduct, and report cost-benefit studies to assess the impact of field-test program(s) in the light of long-range time and social considerations, as well as changing human, system, and societal needs.

Using and Communicating Costs and Impact Data

Make decisions related to necessary future human services and changes in field-tested programs, and communicate these decisions and their rationale to appropriate audiences.

NATURE OF THIS STAFF DEVELOPMENT APPROACH

The topics of our initial 12 staff development modules are listed in Figure 3.1. Central to these topics are the statements of each module's behavioral outcomes, just as statements describing desirable client outcomes are central to the human services program.

Expected Staff Development Outcomes

The outcomes that participants are expected to achieve through this staff development approach are summarized below by module.

MODULE 1—CAREER DEVELOPMENT THEORY.   Participant-expected outcomes include the abilities to:

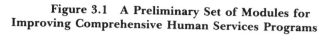

**Figure 3.1   A Preliminary Set of Modules for
Improving Comprehensive Human Services Programs**

1. Identify current practices in your career guidance program that reflect each of the eight career or vocational development theories.
2. For each theory, list at least one additional activity you would consider adding to your program.
3. State the assumptions upon which your current guidance program is based.
4. Produce a written plan which, when implemented, will result in a statement of the philosophy and assumptions underlying the career guidance program you will develop through the course of these modules.

MODULE 2—PROGRAM DEVELOPMENT MODEL. Participant-expected outcomes include the abilities to:

1. List at least three common guidance problems to which the approach described here can help provide solutions.
2. Describe the essential characteristics of the career guidance program improvement approach discussed in the module, and list several of its advantages and disadvantages.
3. List the essential skills to be developed in this staff development program.
4. Identify the skills you want to develop in the staff development program.

MODULE 3—ASSESSING DESIRED OUTCOMES. Participant-expected outcomes include the abilities to:

1. Understand and state the value of assessing the desired outcomes of a program.
2. Specify the tasks and considerations in assessing a program's desired outcomes.
3. Perform basic skills involved in assessing a program's desired outcomes, including:
   a. defining the population(s) and selecting the sample(s).
   b. selecting/developing assessment instruments.
   c. administering instruments.
   d. summarizing and translating data into desired outcomes.
4. Develop a plan for defining the desired outcomes of your program.

MODULE 4—ASSESSING CURRENT STATUS. Participant-expected outcomes include the abilities to:

1. Define "current status assessment," state its emphasis, and explain how it fits into the needs assessment process.
2. State the human, financial, and technical resources of a guidance program.
3. Adapt and/or use an instrument for determining how resources are being used currently.
4. State what techniques are available for assessing current status.
5. Review and select instruments, and items from instruments, for assessing the current status of students according to appropriate criteria.
6. Produce a plan for assessing the current status of your program.

MODULE 5—ESTABLISHING PROGRAM GOALS.   Participant-expected outcomes include the abilities to:

1. Define the phrase "program goal" and give an example of one.
2. Identify program needs by comparing desired outcome and current status information to determine the discrepancies.
3. Draft goals for a program based on the program needs and other relevant information.
4. Classify goals into a useful overall scheme.
5. Determine priorities for the goals of a program.
6. Define issues and techniques important in evaluating and reporting the activities involved in planning career guidance programs.
7. Produce a plan for developing program goals for your program.

MODULE 6—SPECIFYING STUDENT PERFORMANCE OBJECTIVES.

Participant-expected outcomes include the abilities to:

1. State the reasons for and importance of writing career guidance student performance objectives.
2. Write an outcome stating an identifiable performance for a goal statement.
3. Write, or select and modify, a full objective for an outcome. Each such objective will contain the four components of a good objective.
4. Produce a sequenced list of all objectives pertaining to a given goal statement and target population.
5. Produce a plan for developing student performance objectives for your program.

MODULE 7—SELECTING ALTERNATIVE PROGRAM STRATEGIES. Participant-expected outcomes include the abilities to:

1. Write a definition and give three examples of guidance strategies.
2. Write a set of your criteria for considering alternative strategies for guidance objectives.
3. State your decision rule for selecting a strategy to use to reach a guidance objective.
4. Produce a plan for selecting program strategies at your school.

MODULE 8—SPECIFYING PROCESS OBJECTIVES. Participant-expected outcomes include the abilities to:

1. List the advantages of writing process objectives.
2. List process objectives that must be performed in order to implement a given strategy.
3. Assign staff members to carry out process objectives by matching available staff skills with needed skills to accomplish the objectives.
4. Schedule process objectives by use of PERT and by use of time, task, and talent analyses.
5. Incorporate process objectives into planning activities at your school or district.

MODULE 9—DEVELOPING PROGRAM STAFF. Participant-expected outcomes include the abilities to:

1. Use the Skills Checklists to write staff development objectives.
2. Create your own staff development strategies by combining available sources of help with possible delivery methods.
3. Use the criteria suggested in this module and/or your own criteria to select staff development strategies suited to your school or district.
4. Outline the planning and implementation tasks that would need to be completed in your school or district to carry out a given strategy.
5. Map out a plan for developing and administering your own staff development program.

MODULE 10—TRYING OUT ACTIVITIES AND MONITORING. Participant-expected outcomes include the abilities to:

1. State the primary purpose of carrying out preliminary activity tryouts and describe at least two situations in which such pilot testing is useful, and two in which it is a waste of time.
2. Verify the internal logic of a planned career guidance activity, given a written description of such an activity covering its goals, student performance objectives, and process objectives.
3. Develop a relatively accurate estimate of the cost of implementing a career guidance activity.
4. Develop measures of attainment of the process objectives of a career guidance activity, given a written description of the activity and its process objectives.
5. Develop relatively objective, reliable, and valid measures of the outcomes of a career guidance activity.
6. Develop a plan for trying out activities and monitoring early implementation efforts at your school.

MODULE 11—CONDUCTING SUMMATIVE EVALUATION. Participant-expected outcomes include the abilities to:

1. State the purpose and value of conducting a summative evaluation.
2. Select an appropriate evaluation design and sample, given an evaluation situation.
3. Select, adapt, or adopt appropriate measurement instruments, given particular evaluation needs.
4. List the major considerations involved in administering evaluation instruments.
5. Propose appropriate methods for processing, analyzing, and presenting evaluation data.
6. Identify important considerations in determining cost effectiveness.
7. State appropriate decisions based on evaluation results, given an evaluation situation.
8. Map out a plan for conducting a summative evaluation of your program.

MODULE 12—COMMUNICATING EVALUATION RESULTS. Participant-expected outcomes include the abilities to:

1. Explain how content, format, and level of sophistication can vary in an evaluation report.
2. Choose content, format, and level of sophistication appropriate for: (a) decisions and the data they require, (b) audience characteristics, and (c) resources available for producing the evaluation report.
3. Specify how to use simple, logical organization in preparing evaluation reports.
4. Specify how to use concise language in evaluation reports.
5. Specify how to use clear, accurate presentation of data in evaluation reports.
6. Specify appropriate methods that contribute to an interesting, attractive presentation.

7. Tailor your writing and presentation of data to be appropriate for (a) the decisions and data needed for them, (b) audience characteristics, and (c) resources available.

8. Identify the reporting considerations for your own situation and develop a plan for reporting evaluation results using communication strategies appropriate to the considerations you have identified.

Module Objectives and their Purposes

Each module has a set of objectives that incorporate the participant outcomes listed above and serve at least three purposes. First, they direct the module design and writing activities. The module developers do not begin their detailed work on content until its objectives have been agreed upon and stated in the most measurable form possible at that point in the development sequence. Like any behavioral objective, each statement in the set must have four parts: (1) an indication of who should be able to perform the objective (that is easy in this case, since it will be the staff persons experiencing the module); (2) the outcome those persons will be able to perform if they achieve the objective (two types of outcomes, knowledge and skills, are listed in the preceding section); (3) the conditions within which such outcomes will occur; and (4) the standard(s) that will be used to judge the adequacy of the performance. With blueprints shaped around such objectives, module writers and reviewers can direct their efforts at the precise content that will help users accomplish these aims.

A second purpose of module objectives is to serve as guidelines for the learning experiences of the participants. Each module's set is presented in simplified form early in the module. At that point, participants are encouraged to study the objectives closely to determine what they are expected to accomplish in that module. After reviewing the list, if they decide they already have achieved those aims, or are not interested in working on them, the workshop coordinator helps them explore and engage in other staff development options. If they agree that some of the objectives are appropriate for them, they are encouraged to direct their attention only to the module sections that deal with those selected. Since a complete statement of one objective can be lengthy, a list of such statements can be unnecessarily frustrating if it is one of the first things participants encounter when they begin a module. Therefore, the simplified versions presented at the beginning of each module omit the criterion standards used to assess participants' performance. These criteria are provided in a Coordinator's Guide that accompanies each module. Workshop participants interested in receiving these standards before they proceed, or during their work on a module, ask their coordinator to share the set with them.

A third purpose of each set of module objectives entails evaluation. One of the concluding elements of each module is a performance test to help participants and coordinators determine what objectives have been achieved as well as which ones require additional attention. This type of evaluation is strongly learner based. The objectives can also help the developers of the materials and procedures evaluate which parts are working and which ones need further modification. In addition, these objectives can be used to evaluate the long-term effects of the staff development —results that occur after the workshops and that may be different from the immediate effects measured through module tests.

Module Objectives Examples

Two types of objectives, and their component outcomes, are employed in the staff development modules. The first, knowledge objectives, are the ones on which conventional inservice approaches generally focus, if efforts are made to state explicit predetermined objectives for them at all (which is usually not the case). It is the second type, skill objectives, that is the distinctive feature of our staff development. As implied earlier in this chapter, AIR personnel identified critical tasks that experts felt educators needed to perform in order to plan, develop, implement, and evaluate human services programs effectively. Then, the competencies that educators required for successfully conducting these tasks were specified. Next, related competencies were grouped so that a module could be designed for at least two or three of the most fundamental skills in each group. These skills were expressed as competency-based objectives that each module development team could then use to direct their design and writing activities.

The skill type of objectives outlines the most important participant outcomes that each module attempts to achieve. The knowledge objectives summarize selected cognitive outcomes that are prerequisites to the performance of these competencies. Four examples of such knowledge objectives and the modules in which they are found are as follows:

Module 4.   Define "current status assessment," state its emphasis, and explain how it fits into the needs assessment process.

Criterion: The definition should state that the current status assessment determines what a program is and has (i.e., what its resources are and how they are used). The desired outcome assessment determines what an ideal program would be. The discrepancy between these defines the need.

Module 5.   Define the phrase "program goal" and give an example of one.

Criterion: The definition should state that goals are

general statements of program outcomes. They are not specific and behavioral.

A feasible goal should be presented. It should meet the six criteria defined in the module, i.e., be at an appropriate level of generality; be focused on students; be written in clear, direct language; be directed to an outcome, not a process; be suggestive of the types of outcomes to which it will lead; reflect the underlying philosophy and theory intended. Use your judgment in evaluating the example. The last criterion, for example, may be hard to satisfy in a given objective.

Module 6.   State the reasons for and the importance of writing career guidance student performance objectives.

Criterion: The rationale defined should indicate that writing student performance objectives helps structure learning in the program, and facilitates the evaluation of the program. Participants may also indicate original ideas or locally appropriate points.

Module 8.   List the advantages of writing process objectives.

Criterion: Advantages listed should include the fact that they help you to clarify your thinking, replicate the project, report on the project, and manage the project.

In the 12-module series on which this chapter focuses, a competency objective is either an enabler or a terminal type. All of them entail skills that can be operationalized by observable performances, preferably ones indicated by the successful development of a product having measurable relevance for practical settings. We have attempted to concentrate on helping participants internalize skills that are generalizable—ones they can use in practical settings outside the instructional and testing settings provided by the modules. Module 6, for example, contains three competency-based objectives that serve as enablers for the more important fourth, and final, skill. These three are:

1. Write an outcome stating an identifiable performance for a goal statement.

Criteria. The examples provided by the participant must meet these four criteria: Are the outcomes observable performances or behaviors? Are the verbs primarily action verbs? Are the outcomes subject to few interpretations? Do the outcomes actually give evidence that the participant has reached the goal? Is the behavior in the outcome an important or significant one? Is it worth knowing about? Do the outcomes describe what students will be able to do, not what will be done for students?

If any participants fail to meet these criteria, point this out and have them keep working until they can write acceptable examples of outcomes. Each participant must write three correct outcomes in each case.

2. Write, or select and modify, five full objectives from outcomes. Each objective will contain the three components of a good objective.

Criteria. Each of the objectives individually written in Activity 2 must:

indicate the audience to whom it is addressed.

specify the conditions under which it will be evaluated.

indicate the criteria necessary for success.

If any participants fail to include all these parts in their objectives, point out what ones they are omitting and have them keep working until they do complete five acceptable objectives. It may be useful to have participants help each other.

3. Produce a sequenced list of all objectives pertaining to a given goal statement and target population.

Criteria. This outcome is measured three times within

the module: twice in one of the activities and once in the postassessment. In the former instance, two lists of jumbled objectives must be organized and fit into classification schemes, and the correct answers are contained in the criteria. On the postassessment a scheme must be described, a rationale for it provided which is reasonable according to the coordinator's judgment, and a set of objectives previously drafted by the participant arranged within it.

The skills involved in the above three statements are crucial to the construction of measurable objectives that are developmentally sequenced. However, the module attempts to help participants go farther and state such objectives for their own programs. Since participants will not conduct needs activities in their educational settings until after the workshop, they do not have the input data they need to write their program's objectives when they complete this module. Therefore, they check their terminal competence with their workshop coordinator after producing a detailed plan for exactly how they will state their objectives later. The terminal objective related to this competency in Module 6 is as follows:

4.   Produce a plan for developing student performance objectives for your program.
   Criteria. The time and task analysis produced should outline the tasks under each of the major headings listed, assign responsibility for each task to someone, and set a completion date for each task. In addition, the plan should be reasonably:
   logical: Do the tasks flow in logical sequence?
   thorough: Is it detailed enough to be helpful?
   feasible: Is it not too detailed to be burdensome? Are the times allowed for the tasks reasonable?
   fair: Are the responsibilities assigned equitably and fairly?

Module Format

The design specifications of our modules have evolved through pilot (preliminary, small-group) and field (more intensive, large-group) tests in which we have been involved over the last 2 years. Each module is composed of a package of materials including: a consumable module booklet for the participant; a reusable guidebook for each workshop coordinator working with participants on that module; and support materials (e.g., filmstrips, textbooks, journal articles, sample tests, and assessment instruments) referenced to various sections and objectives in the module. Each coordinator's guide contains definitions of the workshop leader's roles and functions and provides information helpful to the performance of those roles.

Each participant's booklet begins with a section that: (1) introduces the general goal and specific participant outcomes of that module; (2) outlines the activities covered by the module, the approximate time that should be allowed for each activity, and the outcomes keyed to each activity; (3) illustrates how the content of this module fits into the comprehensive program planning-evaluation model that serves as the foundation for this staff development series; and (4) provides a glossary defining important terms used in that module.

The four remaining sections include: (1) the main text for in-depth reading interspersed with both questions for group discussion sessions and practice activities; (2) a post-assessment, criterion test for performance feedback to each participant; (3) the aforementioned personal application that encourages participants to apply their acquired knowledge and skills to problems in their local settings; and (4) an appendix of materials helpful throughout the module, including an optional simulation description for discussions of real-life application of the skills; additional readings/materials related to the module's topic; and bibliographic descriptions of key references related to the module's content. Participants' booklets range in length from 40 to 80 pages, with an overall total of approximately 800 pages for the 12 modules.

Format Examples

The table of contents displayed in Chart 3.2 illustrates how the above specifications are integrated with the content to form the participant's booklet for Module 6. For that same module, Chart 3.3 indicates how the participant is apprised of the various module sections, the suggested time intervals for each activity, and the relationship between those activities and that module's five outcomes.

Chart 3.2.   Table of Contents for Module 6

Introduction
Module goal and outcomes
Module outline
Model and Module 6
The Planning
Glossary
Text
Why write objectives
　　Discussion of rationale
Determining student outcomes
　　Types of objectives
　　Specifying outcomes
　　Activity 1—Determining student outcomes
Producing full objectives
　　The audience
　　The behavior
　　The conditions
　　The degree
　　Discussion of factors in objective writing
　　Activity 2—Producing full objectives
Using available banks of objectives
Sequencing objectives
　　Discussion of sequencing and using objectives
　　Activity 3—Sequencing objectives
Postassessment
Application
Appendix
Optional group simulation description
References

Chart 3.3.   Module Outline for Module 6

Approximate time (hours)	Activity	Outcomes
1	*Introduction*	1
	Group activity based on module's goals and outcomes. The coordinator will explain the structure and purposes of the module. Questions and discussion included. Tape-slide presentation.	
3 1/2	*Text*	1–5
	Presentation of the important information related to writing objectives. Discussion sessions and practice activities interspersed.	
1/2	*Postassessment*	1–4
	Assessment of your acquired knowledge and skills.	
1	*Application*	5
	Planning for the use of these abilities in your own setting.	

Two other participant booklet sections that probably should be illustrated are the practice activities that follow the short reading topics in the text, and the personal application that serves as the important conclusion to each module. Chart 3.4 provides an example of one of the three activity exercises contained in Module 6. It asks workshop participants to practice analyzing and writing student objectives. For that same module, Chart 3.5 illustrates how we use the "Application" section in each module to encourage participants to apply the skills they have acquired to program development problems in their own school situations. The coordinator for this module assesses participants' completed products of this personal application. This assessment process determines the degree to which they have demonstrated the terminal skills of the module, provides constructive feedback to help them bring their performance to an acceptable level, and certifies when that level has been attained and all module objectives have been met.

Inservice Pilot Tests

During the 1974–75 school year, this staff development approach was pilot tested in a 3-day workshop setting with 16 counselors from the San Francisco Bay Area. At the same time the 12 modules received a professional review from staff members in the Guidance Division of the California State Department of Education, as well as five national experts in the field of guidance, counseling, placement, and followthrough. The purpose of this pilot test and professional review was to collect feedback on each staff development module and the overall workshop procedures (e.g., participants' selection of modules, coordinator's roles, module testing activities). The information collected was then used to make improvements in all materials and procedures so that extensive field tests with larger groups and more detailed follow-up evaluations could be scheduled for late summer, 1975.

The results of these trial attempts were essentially positive. However, sufficient constructive reactions were obtained to warrant a major revision. We classified these criticisms into two categories. The first group included the concerns participants had relating to this type of individualized, competency-based, staff development workshop. This was a novel experience for them and not one for which they felt well prepared, from the standpoint of both knowledge and motivation. The second category of concerns focused on the delivery system we used in the workshops. The materials needed to be more palatable to the participants and more self-motivating. To respond to the first

Chart 3.4   Activity 2—Producing Full Objectives
(Module 6)

As a group, determine if any of the four components are missing in the following "objectives." After each statement below, write "A," "B," "C," and/or "D," depending on what is missing. Write "None" if all the components are present.

1. The tenth-grade student will have an awareness of the changes in sex stereotypes in occupational choices.
2. To be able to describe the difference between an ability and an interest in a written paragraph which will be evaluated by the teacher.
3. When given a list of occupations, all third-grade students will be able to identify those which are service occupations.
4. In a 15- to 20-minute interview with the counselor, graduating seniors will be able to describe their plans for the first year out of high school. Each senior must indicate to the counselor's satisfaction that s/he has carefully considered available alternatives for post-high school education and training.

For each "objective" above which is missing one or more components, rewrite it (as a group) to include all components.

Now, working individually, write an objective for each of the following student outcomes.

1. tell in her/his own words the difference in working conditions s/he observed in different parts of the plant
2. is able to select two persons from history and discuss why s/he would like to emulate them
3. can identify most occupations in the community
4. can state important self-characteristics
5. can select important criteria of job for own satisfaction

For each of the objectives, underline the audience or target population once, the test conditions twice, and the degree or criteria three times. (The behavior or outcome will not be underlined.)

Chart 3.5   Application for Module 6

You are now ready to map out a plan for applying the skills you developed in this module to your own setting. Thinking of the sections of the module and the questions you have discussed, consider the tasks that must be accomplished to generate and sequence student performance objectives for your program, the person who should be primarily responsible for each task, and the date by which the task should be done.

Since student performance objectives must be written after the goals have been established, and before strategies for meeting the goals and objectives are determined, the dates you choose must coordinate with those set for other program-planning tasks. If possible, this exercise should be done under the direction of someone from your district who would be good at taking charge of this effort and who would like to do it. In the space provided, list your tasks, the people responsible, and the completion dates, using the major headings that are already noted. Use additional paper as needed.

Tasks	Individual(s) responsible	Completion date
1. Establish in the necessary people the motivation to specify student performance objectives for the career guidance program. (More space is provided in the participant's booklet for each of these sections.)		
2. Determine student outcomes for the program.		
3. Produce full objectives for the student outcomes.		
4. Establish and use a sensible sequencing system for the objectives.		

category, we decided to devote more effort to interviewing potential participants before the beginning of the work-shop and then orienting those who want to participate and are selected. This additional effort would attempt to: (1) convey fully the advantages and disadvantages of the program planning and evaluation model that this set of modules stresses; (2) identify our staff development assumptions, and convey them to participants before the selection; (3) explain just how much hard work is involved and the kind of commitment that this staff development approach demands: and (4) select highly motivated participants.

On the other hand, the following major actions are being taken to revise module format and content to effect an improved delivery system:

1. Edit each participant booklet to make it simpler and more streamlined.
2. Produce an improved Module 2, relying more on a tape-slide introduction, verbal presentations, and discussion, and less on reading.
3. Change the format to have smaller sections of reading, with each followed by a brief discussion period and the activity pertaining to that section.
4. Change the preassessments into outlines of each module, useful as prereading aids.
5. Modify the simulation so that either a hypothetical case study is available or participants can use their own school setting for the discussion.
6. Spread the exercises through the text, leave in only essential ones, personalize them where possible, and call them activities.
7. Move the discussion questions relating to participants' own setting in the Application section to the appropriate section of reading. Leave the task of mapping out a plan for using the skills in the present Application.
8. Make the Glossary more accessible; expand this where necessary.
9. Improve layouts of all materials. Add boldface type and boxes. Use color-coded pages for discussions and activities.

10. Thoroughly edit all modules to eliminate jargon, lighten the tone, and clarify the style.
11. Add more examples, summaries, textual humor, and cartoons.
12. Segment, expand, and professionalize the tape-slide presentation.
13. Make fuller use of coordinators in conveying the basic idea of each module.

The above modifications are being implemented to ensure better products for the field test scheduled in late summer 1975. We believe the pilot test and professional review helped us provide an improved staff development approach for this set of modules and for any subsequent pre- and inservice staff work we attempt. Hopefully, other educators of human services personnel will be able to profit from our learning experiences, too. A few of the recommendations we would make to these educators are summarized in the next section.

RECOMMENDATIONS TO STAFF DEVELOPERS

Many of the pitfalls we experienced undoubtedly are not unique to this type of modularized, competency-based staff development approach. Because we believe that we have learned some generalizations that would apply equally to your staff education setting, we express them as recommendations for your consideration:
1. It is important that participants in such workshops receive an early orientation to the purposes and procedures of the subsequent training experiences.
2. Each module should be short and succinct.
3. Reading should be kept to a minimum.
4. Unnecessary jargon should be eliminated.

5. Preassessment activities should be carefully designed, if used at all. The ones we used to help participants determine their knowledge levels before they started major module activities were too specific to the module content and were too frustrating since participants invariably could not answer the questions correctly.
6. Similar caution should be adopted if simulation activities are included. We used them to help participants practice their skills on a predetermined practical problem for which correct solutions could be developed. However, they seemed too "canned." Participants were more anxious to practice on their own school problems than on contrived examples.
7. All referenced materials should be easily integrated into the participants' booklets so that access to them is not too cumbersome and confusing.
8. Personal application exercises should be spaced throughout each module. Initially, we placed these applications at the end of each module. However, we learned that this delayed them too long. Participants wanted to apply their module competencies to their own school settings much earlier in each module.

PROBLEMS WITH THIS STAFF DEVELOPMENT APPROACH

Even after reading the preceding section, in case you still are convinced that this approach does not involve major problems, we decided to conclude this chapter with a brief review of some of the more critical issues with which we continue to battle. These issues are not ones for which we can make general recommendations at this time, as we have done in the above section. However, we summarized these concerns here because we think they have general relevance to any staff development program. In addition, we hope their discussion will facilitate the planning activities of other researchers and educators who are exploring similar staff development alternatives.

The most nagging concern we have faced throughout all aspects of our research and development in this area entails participant motivation. Most of our participants to date have experienced our approach in an inservice setting. Our current perceptions are that many such personnel are accustomed to staff development activities in which they (a) do not have to be too actively involved; (b) do not have to work too hard; (c) can be entertained by powerful speakers and glossy audio-visual and printed materials; (d) can spend a lot of time talking in group discussions; (e) have few reading and product development tasks requested of them; (f) can follow workshop leaders who assume a controlling role; and (g) are not accountable for increments in the workshop performance.

As we hope it is obvious from the preceding sections of this chapter, the delivery system of our staff development approach contradicts most of these preferences. This approach attempts to engage participants in a learning process that emphasizes: (a) individualization; (b) learner responsibility for personal growth; (c) more independent, self-instructional activities than many participants desire and are accustomed to; (d) participant generation of specific products that will have transfer value to their practical settings after the workshops; (e) few didactic presentations and lectures and more reading and self-study activities; (f) a facilitator, rather than a leader, role for workshop coordinators; and (g) performance assessment of gains participants make in their knowledge and skills as a result of these learning experiences. Needless to say, we have experienced motivational problems with many of our participants. In response, we have modified our delivery system as much as possible so that we can maintain the learning principles in which we believe. At the same time, we are committed to a mission of trying gradually to change participants' staff development expectations to more specific, measurable, and higher goals than they have adopted in the past.

A related problem with our delivery system is the amount of participant instructional time it requires. This type of modularized approach reinforces individualization of learning experiences to the needs and characteristics of learners; but because it is designed and evaluated on the basis of measurable objectives, it also requires that participants receive specified learning resources to achieve agreed-upon performance levels. The instructional materials and procedures have to "deliver." Therefore, participant time for exposure to appropriate learning experiences becomes a very important ingredient. We began with modules that necessitated 10 to 15 hours of learner time. Even though, as was mentioned in Chapter 2, we have tried to extinguish all attempts to present our program planning-evaluation model as a lock-step series of sequentially related activities, we have had to deviate from this goal in our staff development. We know that participants who are beginning their experience with this model must first be exposed to certain fundamental concepts before they work on some of the more sophisticated skills. This meant that each participant agreed to take three or four modules. The total time commitment became impossible in many human services settings. As a result we have reduced the module time for the typical participant: the average time is now 6 hours per module. However, for inservice education we continue to ask each participant to commit to at least three modules. Therefore, this staff development approach is not feasible for human services personnel who cannot devote at least 4 days of learning time to the process.

A third problem also relates to motivation and time issues. This entails participants' reluctance to engage in evaluation activities aimed either at helping them assess changes in their performance levels or at assisting us to improve the staff development materials and procedures.

Usually, they have been more supportive of the second evaluation purpose than they have of the first. A central concept in our approach is a dedication to specifying instructional objectives and measuring progress toward them. However, many of our participants have not shared that dedication. Some of them seemed to have felt threatened, particularly by any preassessment activities intended to help them assess changes in their performance. They were demoralized by their entry level assessment results and frustrated that our items were tailored far too closely to module content. As a result, we have abandoned the preassessments and are focusing more attention on criterion-referenced evaluations at the end, and after, the workshop. Other participants, anxious to emphasize learning experiences that had immediate application to their practical job settings, felt that evaluation activities diverted them from this main purpose. We have therefore reduced the number and extent of the evaluation instruments and procedures but also have reaffirmed our dedication to trying to stimulate participants to adopt more positive attitudes to the aims, process, and results of the evaluation of any staff development approach.

The most important aspect of evaluation of our staff development is the measurement of changes in participants' competencies. Solid criterion-referenced evaluation requires that skill-based objectives be assessed by instruments and activities that ask participants to demonstrate their performance of competencies outlined in those objectives, and the products that result from this performance. Because our approach stresses the acquisition and practice of competencies that are transferable beyond the staff development setting into each participant's practical job setting, pencil-and-paper measurement items will not suffice. Indeed, we gave up our earlier emphasis on assessing each participant's competence in solving contrived problems through simulation experiences. One reason for this change was participants' concern about the artificiality of the simulations and their preference for more personally relevant assessments. We are now concentrating on the personal application plans described earlier in this chapter, and postworkshop follow-up evaluations of the degree to which such plans are implemented. However, this tactic incurs the participant time problem again and is expensive to conduct. Obviously, we have not completely resolved our competency evaluation problem.

The final issue entails our desire to produce staff development training that is equally appropriate for preservice and inservice settings. Thus far, most of our efforts have concentrated on inservice education. However, we are fully aware of some critical issues involved in generalizing our staff development approach to college and university programs. Some of the strategies that need to be worked out include:

1. Strategies for conducting tasks and competency analysis for determining generic human service skills
2. Strategies for conducting competency assessments to determine:
   a. what students to admit to human services education at the graduate and undergraduate level
   b. how to develop individualized programs of study tailored to the interests and needs of each student accepted
3. Consistent procedures and formats to be used by all department members in the competency training of these students
4. Strategies for performance evaluation of student progress on individualized programs of study
5. Strategies for changing state credentialing requirements to be compatible with a competency-based certification model developed through such an educational program

6. Strategies for implementing information management services to support such competency-based learning
7. Strategies for follow-up evaluation of the job performance of graduates and, therefore, the human services educational program
8. Maintaining recurrent task and competency analyses to ensure that such programs focus on current competencies appropriate to practical settings

We do not expect to solve these issues without a heavy commitment, but we do anticipate working on them over the next few years.

SUMMARY

This chapter reported the procedures and results of our recent attempts to develop, pilot test, revise, and field test a competency-based staff development approach. Different components and products used in this staff development alternative were illustrated. This approach aims at helping human services personnel acquire and practice identifiable knowledge outcomes and skills they need in order to plan, develop, implement, and evaluate social action and educational programs by employing the systematic model and process briefly reviewed in Chapter 2.

Also discussed here were recommendations for improving this staff development approach, as well as unresolved problems involved in its implementation and evaluation. Possible solutions to these problems were suggested. The need for integrating this type of inservice staff education with preservice programs was discussed, as were obstacles that may hamper such articulation attempts.

The next chapter addresses the need for client programs that are compatible with the Chapter 2 planning-evaluation model and the Chapter 3 staff development approach. Example strategies and materials used in a small sample of such programs are presented in summary form. Resource persons who can provide further information are indicated for each program introduced.

This chapter deals with the process of selecting and developing guidance and educational activities for clients. The process constitutes the second phase (program development) of the systematic planning-evaluation model introduced in Chapter 2 and summarized in Chart 2.1. Some existing client programs are described as examples of this phase as outlined in Chart 2.2. The programs selected are only illustrative and not exhaustive.

Chapter 4

USING COMPETENCY-BASED CLIENT STRATEGIES AND MATERIALS

Program strategies, materials, activities, and curriculum for clients are means to ends. They are methods or procedures for accomplishing certain goals or objectives. Before you determine what methods or procedures to use with clients (or what curriculum to write or what materials to select), you should preface that decision with the planning-evaluation process detailed in the last three chapters.

Consider, for example, the "counselors counsel" attitude discussed in Chapter 1. Individual counseling (one-to-one relationship) is a strategy for achieving some purposes. It is a method, a procedure, an activity, a means to an end. It is also what most counselors are trained to do and what they want to do; in fact, most counselors feel it is their "purpose" for being hired. In a sense, counseling becomes the end. Often school-based programs reflect this attitude in counseling handbooks. Typical statements read as follows:

Every student will receive individual counseling.

Each student will be counseled individually at least twice every semester.

Counselors will spend at least 50% of their time counseling students individually.

Unless the planning-evaluation process precedes the selection of human services strategies or activities, it is difficult to determine their value. In other words, unless it is first known what outcomes are desired, it is difficult (or impossible) to determine whether counselors' individual counseling with students is a valuable use of time. Is individual counseling likely to achieve the desired outcome? Is it more likely to achieve the desired outcome than are other methods? Does the guidance staff have the skills to use other methods?

Selecting and/or developing activities for clients, therefore, is part of a total process of planning, developing, implementing, and evaluating. When human services personnel decide to counsel, lead groups, present a curriculum, set up a career center, provide job placement, or offer any services to clients, they are choosing from a variety of possible strategies that they hope will accomplish something. Obviously, this decision (selection of a strategy) will be more productive if it is based upon criteria more precise than "hope" and "something."

The previous chapters have described the need for and the skills involved in developing this precision. Clearly established needs, program goals, and performance objectives will define the "something to be accomplished" and will make it easier to determine the likelihood of success beyond hope. Nevertheless, selecting the "best" strategy to use presents some other decision problems.

In addition to the questions already raised, as a program developer you face an additional serious problem. In order to choose a best strategy, you must know about several alternative "good" strategies from which to choose. Knowing a number of good strategies is a major problem.

Today, many new strategies are on the "market." These include interpersonal techniques (human relations skills, value clarification, assertiveness training, etc.) as well as "packaged curriculum" for clients (programmed materials, multimedia, etc.). Counselors, teachers, and others also have written their own materials or have adapted published materials for their use. But even with clearly defined purposes and objectives, a counselor may fail to choose a certain strategy or set of materials simply because it is not known.

The rest of this chapter lists some sources of human services strategies and provides some details on a few examples. (Those strategies selected are only illustrations and in no way are intended to be an exhaustive list of resources.) They have been tailored to students in school settings; however, they also should provide illustrations for human services personnel working in other educational and social agencies. The examples and the list of sources may help in knowing about existing guidance strategies. They do not help in knowing how to choose the "best" strategy. Knowing how to choose strategies and materials is a process that involves basic skills and competencies that need to be added to those discussed in the first three chapters.

As a program developer, when you look for the means to achieve the objectives of a well-planned program, you would like to be able to consider an array of possible strategies where the following kind of data are available:

1. What outcomes does this strategy attempt to achieve?
2. What target populations does it serve?
3. What staff, facilities, materials, and time are needed?

4. What procedures are used?
5. How well does it achieve the outcomes?
6. Where can I find out more about it?

Unfortunately, strategies and materials for human services are not normally researched, designed, and packaged in ways that make these answers easily available to program developers. On the other hand, the answers to many of these questions may be idiosyncratic to your own setting. Therefore, you may need to find some answers locally.

Likewise, since a well-planned program in a particular district or locale probably will require the development of tailormade strategies, some adaption, modification, and/or supplementation of published programs will, no doubt, be required. However, what follows should be useful when you reach the stage of selecting strategies.

Several guidance strategies and sets of materials are discussed as examples of human development programs that are available to education and guidance personnel. Those selected for illustration are examples of programs that might be useful as means to achieving goals and objectives in the general domain of career education and career guidance. At the end of this chapter, an annotated listing of resources for additional suggestions is included.

EXAMPLE PROGRAMS

Seven student programs will be reviewed. The following format will be used in order to provide some uniformity to the review and to help provide the kind of answers you and other program developers will seek when selecting strategies. The resource person is listed for cases where more extensive information about the total published program may be desired.

Overview: What it is, intended target population, and materials involved

Goals
and objectives: The stated purposes and objectives—examples when available

Procedures,
methodology: What is done, staff requirement, time involved, and community involvement

Evaluation: What research was conducted; what results were achieved

Source
of information: Person or agency to consult for more information

LIFE CAREER DEVELOPMENT SYSTEM
HUMAN DEVELOPMENT SERVICES

Overview

The Life Career Development System (LCDS) consists of six interrelated components that together make up a dynamic program of career development. The LCDS is concerned with the development of the total individual and encompasses education, occupation, and leisure time. Career decisions and plans are seen in this system as life decisions and plans, and they are considered as an integrated developmental sequence involving the goals, values, plans, and decisions of the individual now and in the future. The program is designed for students from junior high school through college and adult.

The six components are as follows: (1) nine career development modules of student learning experiences; (2) a facilitator's resource bank; (3) a participant's journal; (4) pre- and postevaluation measures; (5) a facilitator's training workshop (required of leaders); and (6) a LCDS user communication network for sharing across the country.

Goals and Objectives

Each of the nine career development modules includes a statement of purpose, a list of broad goals, and a brief description of the focus and activity for each session. This outline is listed below for Module 4, "Expanding Options."

PURPOSE.   The purpose of this module is to broaden participants' perceptions of the world of work by helping them to understand the reasons behind the emergence of new career roles, to evaluate changing work values, to develop increased sensitivity to the social consequences of career choice, and to become more aware of the wide variety of options available to them.

GOALS.   The main goals of this module are to help participants:

1. Increase their understanding of new career roles and the reasons for their emergence in today's world
2. Clarify personal work values
3. Identify work values being expressed through new career roles
4. Become aware of and sensitive to the nature of resistance to new career roles
5. Develop greater understanding of the social consequences of various work roles
6. Broaden their thinking about the kinds of career options available to them

OBJECTIVES.   Participants will be able to do the following:

1. Describe six new career roles which have emerged in recent years
2. Identify four reasons for the emergence of new career roles
3. Identify two work values being expressed in two new career roles
4. Discuss ways in which their holding a specific work value might enhance and enrich their lives or cause them difficulties in the future
5. Write a letter of application for employment, incorporating their reasons for wanting the position (their values)
6. State three specific kinds of resistance which may be encountered by persons entering nontraditional careers
7. List the possible social consequences of two work roles

Procedures, Methodology

The LCDS is focused primarily on participant learning and outcomes. A four-step learning model is utilized which involves: (1) self-interest arousal regarding goals and objectives; (2) experience-based learning of life career development tasks and problems; (3) personalization of learning to participants' own needs, values, and lifestyle preferences; (4) behavioral try-out of new learning and competencies in real life situations.

The six components of the system provide program developers or leaders with all materials, instructions, and even leadership skill training. These components are more fully described below:

1. NINE CAREER DEVELOPMENT MODULES.   Each module consists of from six to nine 50-minute sessions comprising individual and group structured learning experiences that may be used daily, weekly, in a concentrated unit, or spread

over a semester or a year. All modules are presented by a trained career development facilitator who coordinates the learning experiences of the participants.

2. FACILITATOR'S RESOURCE BANK.   Each facilitator is provided with a two-volume Facilitator's Resource Bank that gives (1) detailed instructions for each module session; (2) warm-up exercises; (3) specific suggestions for use at different age levels; and (4) enrichment resources. Worksheets are provided so that the module handbooks may be used repeatedly.

3. PARTICIPANT'S JOURNAL.   Participants compile their own journals as they move through the modules. These provide an ongoing record of personal experiences, reactions, and insights as they experiment with new learning and behaviors. Journals are a useful vehicle for reference and for sharing new knowledge and discussing its implications with peers and parents.

4.PRE/POST LEARNING MEASURES.   Each participant responds to a number of situations before beginning the modules and again at the conclusion as a way of measuring growth in knowledge, skills, and attitudes. These pre/post measures provide feedback to the individual participant concerning what s/he has gained from the program, as well as group "assessment data" useful to educational and community decisionmakers.

5. FACILITATOR'S TRAINING WORKSHOP.   All career development specialists participate in a special training workshop which familiarizes them with the module content and helps them to understand and acquire skill in presenting the various learning activities of the modules to the participants. Emphasis is given to helping facilitators acquire a basic conceptual approach to career development which is consistent with that used in the modules.

6. LCDS USER COMMUNICATION NETWORK. The LCDS has been and is now being used in a variety of settings and with varied groups across the country. To insure that the experiences and ideas of previous and present users are optimally utilized, a communication network of users has been established that provides for regular sharing of experiences. Through this ongoing sharing, LCDS users have a chance to renew or refresh their approaches and resources.

Evaluation

Participant feedback for local evaluation purposes is provided in the pre/post learning measures.

LCDS is now in the process of being formally evaluated, but initial data seem to indicate that it is an effective vehicle for positive personal growth. For details of evaluation results write to the person listed below.

Contact:

Dr. Garry Walz
Human Development Services, Inc.
P. O. Box 1403
Ann Arbor, Michigan 48106

BREAD AND BUTTERFLIES
A CURRICULUM GUIDE IN CAREER DEVELOPMENT, 1974 AGENCY FOR INSTRUCTIONAL TELEVISION

Overview

This is a "project" in career development for 9- to 12-year-olds. The project includes fifteen 15-minute color television programs, a curriculum guide, an inservice teachers' program, and workshop materials.

Goals and Objectives

Eight broad goals are listed for the entire series of 15 programs. Each program has a lesson goal and a list of intended student outcomes. The project goals and those for one program, "Decisions—Decisions" are listed below.

PROJECT GOALS.   The full implementation of *Bread and Butterflies* (with its accompanying classroom materials and activities) will help students to:

1. Develop a clearer, more positive understanding of self —their interests, abilities, values, and interpretations of the events in their lives
2. Exert greater control over their lives through decision-making and planning
3. Develop personal and interpersonal skills and attitudes essential to success in school and work
4. Develop greater respect for other people and the work they do
5. Develop a clearer concept of successful work behavior —the attitudes, skills, and responsibilities demonstrated by successful people at school and at work
6. Develop skills necessary to gather, process, and act upon information about self in relation to a constantly changing work environment
7. Relate their immediate experiences and decisions to their evolving career development
8. See the connection between school and the real world; understand the relationship between what they learn in school and the problems and activities outside the school

LESSON #4 (EXAMPLE LESSON):   Decisions—Decisions
Program Goal. This goal is to help students apply the decisionmaking process by selecting and explaining a number

of hypothetical options; and to help them discover factors that influence decisions and possible present and future consequences of given decisions.

Example Program Outcomes. As a result of the lesson, students should:

1. Recognize that usually they have to make choices about what they do
2. Be able to identify a process for making decisions
3. Be able to project the possible consequences of various options that affect a decision

Procedures, Methodology

The programs offer brief dramatized versions of the key concepts, while the guide shows how the concept can be translated into classroom activities and related to curriculum areas, especially language arts, mathematics, science, and social studies.

Suggested techniques (adult interviews, on-the-job observations, workers as resource persons, home projects, etc.) involve community and school interaction. Applied learning activities are also presented.

Evaluation

The project evaluation was conducted by the Educational Testing Service at Princeton, New Jersey, under the direction of Dr. Saul Rockman of the Agency for Instructional Television. In 1975 a utilization research survey was conducted in Santa Clara County in California. *Bread and Butterflies* was used as an inservice training activity for teachers.

Most teachers view *Bread and Butterflies* as a single class activity (81%), and 94% indicated that they either always (44%) or often (50%) follow *Bread and Butterflies* with a discussion or further activity. The reinforcement activities related to *Bread and Butterflies* usually last less than 15 minutes, but sometimes from 15 to 30 minutes. More than half (61%) of the teachers said they have the teacher's manual for *Bread and Butterflies,* and almost all of the manual users found it helpful for using the series.

Contact:

Agency for Instructional Television
Box A
Bloomington, Indiana 47401

CAREER EDUCATION AND SATELLITE TECHNOLOGY DEMONSTRATION, 1974
THE FEDERATION OF ROCKY MOUNTAIN STATES, DENVER, COLORADO

Overview

This is a federally funded project to demonstrate the feasibility and acceptability of a satellite-based media distribution system using a variety of program materials in career education. Fifty-six junior high schools in eight states participated. The program consists of 71 video broadcasts (35 minutes each), student booklets, a teacher's guide, and a series of 16 hour-long broadcasts of inservice programs for teachers.

Goals and Objectives

The overall purpose of the program is "to provide the student with the skills needed to make positive and logical decisions about his or her education and career based on solid self-knowledge and information about the world of work." Each of the 71 student broadcasts has a goal statement and a series of activities designed to achieve the goal.

Twenty-eight student objectives are also listed. Following is a sample of 15:

1. Student recognition and acquisition of decision-making skills: collecting information; considering alternatives; considering outcomes, risk-taking and probabilities, strategies
2. Student recognition of how assessment affects alternatives
3. Student recognition of many reasons why people work
4. Student identification of some of her/his aptitudes as part of self-assessment
5. Student identification of some of her/his temperaments as part of self-assessment
6. Student exploration of many careers and some aptitudes, interests, and temperaments needed for specific occupational examples from the following *Dictionary of Occupational Titles* (DOT) categories:
    Farming, Fishery, and Forestry Occupations
    Structural Trades
    Technical, Managerial, and Professional Occupations
    Machine Trades
    Service Occupations
    Clerical and Sales Occupations
    Processing Occupations
    Bench Trades
    Miscellaneous Occupations
7. Student exploration of how lifestyle preferences can affect career alternatives
8. Student exploration of how training and/or education can affect career alternatives
9. Student recognition of the concepts of occupational mobility and specialization

10. Student recognition of interests as defined by the DOT and interests needed in specific occupations

11. Student exploration of the physical demands and working conditions associated with a variety of occupations

12. Student recognition of the history of unions and how they work today

13. Student recognition that social and cultural changes affect employment

14. Student exploration of self-employment possibilities

15. Student exploration of the skills required to be a knowledgeable consumer

Procedures, Methodology

Programs are broadcast every day to receiving classrooms via satellite. Following the teacher's guide and utilizing the student booklets, teachers follow up with activities, discussions, and assignments. Regular classroom teachers participate and may use as little or as much additional time as desired. The community is involved to the extent that teachers follow the community-based activities suggested.

Topics of the program include self-assessment, values and strategies in decision making, information about occupations in the DOT, how ecology and environment impact on careers, unions, job security, leisure, effects of social and cultural changes on the world of work.

Evaluation

Evaluation is now being conducted on both the use of technology and the achievement of program objectives. Field-test research was conducted on all aspects prior to the experimental year 1974–75. For information regarding the

availability of evaluation results, write to the person listed
below.

Contact:

Dr. Al McWilliams
Content Coordinator
Satellite Technology Demonstration
Federation of Rocky Mountain States
Suite 300 B
2480 West 26th Avenue
Denver, Colorado 80211

DECISIONS AND OUTCOMES, 1973
COLLEGE ENTRANCE EXAMINATION BOARD, NEW YORK

Overview

This is a program designed to teach senior-high and col-
lege-age students the skills of decision making. It is packaged in the form of a student booklet with a leader's guide.
This version is a follow-up publication to *Deciding,* a similar
program for junior-high students.

Goals and Objectives

The content of the program is divided into three major
units or purposes:

1. The examination and recognition of personal values
2. Knowledge and use of adequate, reliable information
3. Knowledge and use of an effective strategy for action

Each unit is a series of exercises, activities, and discussions with its own purpose or objective. Some examples
are: definition of what makes decisions important; distinc-

tion between a good decision and a good outcome; recognition of the importance of values in the decision process; recognition of the relation between values and behavior; precision in writing objectives; understanding of risk-taking in decisionmaking; information-collecting skills; utilizing experience as information; predicting possible outcomes.

Procedures, Methodology

This program is designed as a curriculum to be taught in group guidance or classroom sessions from short mini-courses to full-semester courses. A leader skilled in group leadership is required. Training sessions for leaders are provided by the College Entrance Examination Board.

The procedures involve simulations, role-playing, group exercises, and discussions. Individual activities are suggested and other sources of group activities are cited. The student workbook is not intended to be a lock-step curriculum but a guide to student activities. The Leader's Guide provides precise directions for each exercise as well as suggestions for adaptations.

Evaluation

"Feedback" activities, both formal and informal, are suggested in the Leader's Guide as a kind of evaluation for leaders. Other, more precise, evaluation measures would come from assessment of the degree to which leader's objectives were attained. However, instruments are included in the Guide for process evaluation, middle and early course evaluation, and end-of-course evaluation.

Decisions and Outcomes is built upon the success of *Deciding*, which was published and evaluated earlier. For a report of an evaluation conducted with student users see "Students Evaluate Deciding" by Gordon P. Miller, in *College Board Review No. 86, 1972.*

Contact:

Mr. Gordon Miller
Program Service Officer
College Entrance Examination Board
888 Seventh Avenue
New York, New York 10019

CAREER GUIDANCE, COUNSELING AND PLACEMENT GUIDE AND CAREER EDUCATION METHODS AND PROCESSES, 1974
THE CURATORS OF THE UNIVERSITY OF MISSOURI COLUMBIA, MISSOURI

Overview

Elements of an Illustrative Program Guide is a systematic collection of suggestions to assist leaders to develop and implement career guidance, counseling, and placement programs.

Concepts, goals, and objectives, and procedures for achieving them are discussed and outlined for grades kindergarten through 12. Chapters I and II provide a rationale and a model for program development. Two appendixes contain examples of goals, objectives, sample activities, and selected resources.

Methods and Processes is a companion set of materials consisting of two major components: a methods and processes guide and a systematically organized series of teaching modules for grades kindergarten through 12.

Goals and Objectives

The *Illustrative Program Guide* speaks to the sequential relationships that exist between concepts, goals, objectives, and activities. These activities become the processes through which goals and objectives are attained. Objectives and activities are broken down into age or grade levels: K–3, 4–6, 7–9, 10–12. An example of one concept is provided in Chart 4.1.

Chart 4.1

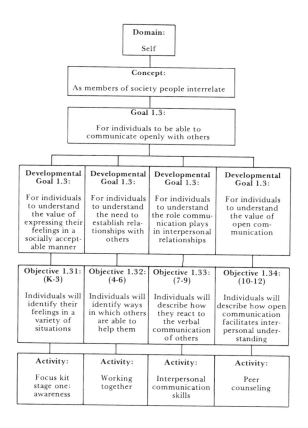

The following is an example of objectives and learner activities found in one module from the *Career Education Methods and Processes.* The module is entitled "You: Who, Where, When" and is for developmental level 4–6.

Learning sequence number three:

A. *Objectives*
    The learner will differentiate between natural and cri-
    sis events. The learner will describe himself or herself
    in terms of "happenings" and how he or she has
    changed throughout life.

B. *Sequence Overview*
    The term "events" when used to designate an ele-
    ment of one's career includes both natural events that
    make up the stages of a life span and events that may
    be considered crisis or once-in-a-lifetime happenings.
    Within this module, attention is focused on awareness
    of time and change. The learner will better under-
    stand the meaning of an event, or occurrence, by
    looking at the ensuing effects—time, growth, change,
    development.

C. *Learner Activities*
    A record of our year—a classroom scrapbook-diary
    Patterns—rhythmic movement, role-playing, oral ex-
    pression
    What is a time line?—interviewing to develop a per-
    son's time line of life
    My own time line—develop time line of my entire life

Procedures, Methodology, and Evaluation

Because the *Illustrative Program Guide* is a collection of suggested student activities designed to meet certain objectives, the procedures and methodology depend on which
activities are chosen. Activities range from teacher-led discussions to using the DOT, to role-playing, peer counseling, community interviewing, and postsecondary placement procedures.

Evaluation procedures involved the revision of the
Guide through review by expert consultants from May 1973
to the present publication.

The *Career Education Methods and Processes* student modules include developmental learning activities based on the Career Education Model described earlier. Methods include such activities and exercises as infusing values clarification, creating and facilitating classroom climate, discussion groups, role-playing, and world of work exploration. Since most of the modules are in the initial stages of development, no evaluation data are currently available on them.

Contact:

Drs. Norman Gysbers and Earl Moore, Editors
One Hill Hall
University of Missouri
Columbia, Missouri 65201

BALTIMORE PLACEMENT AND FOLLOW-UP PROGRAM
CASE STUDIES IN PRACTICAL CAREER GUIDANCE, NUMBER 1.
JUNE 1973, AMERICAN INSTITUTES FOR RESEARCH

Overview

This program provides placement and follow-up services to all graduates and dropouts in the city's public secondary schools. Central office coordinators offer the service and make available a variety of occupational guidance materials to students. About one-half (4000) of the graduates and dropouts take advantage of these services and materials. Work-study programs are an additional service.

Goals and Objectives

The program lists 38 aims and objectives, phrased in terms of what the coordinators will do. For example:

1. To make students aware of the free service placement
2. To assist students in vocational and occupational information
3. To assist students to make adjustments during their initial job entry

The student outcome expected is that each participant will find employment commensurate with his/her abilities and interests.

Procedures, Methodology

Thirty-five placement coordinators are employed in the secondary schools and education centers and by the central office. The central staff is led by the Department Head of Placement who is supervised by the Supervisor of Job-Oriented Programs and Placement. The central office staff also includes coordinators of (1) distributive education and food services, (2) apprenticeship programs, and (3) health careers. Placement has been an objective of the guidance division in Baltimore since 1928.

Students are acquainted with services through assemblies and closed meetings. Many students also participate in job-readiness sessions taught by coordinators. Coordinators contact and work with employers and develop close cooperation with civic and community organizations.

Evaluation

Yearly program evaluation reveals that approximately 75% of students seeking full-time placement are placed. In 1971–72 there were 3626 full-time placements as a result of the program. In addition, 2417 part-time placements and 2526 temporary and summer placements brought the total number of placements that year to 8569.

Every student is contacted at intervals of 3 months, 6 months, and 1 year after placement. Follow-up with employers is also conducted.

Contact:

For more information, the entire case study report can be found in Educational Resources Information Center (ERIC) (ED 076 927).

or write to:

Department Head
Placement and Follow-up Program
Baltimore Public Schools
Baltimore, Maryland 21218

JOB DEVELOPMENT PROGRAM—CLEVELAND PUBLIC SCHOOLS
CASE STUDIES IN PRACTICAL CAREER GUIDANCE, NUMBER 9
JUNE 1973, AMERICAN INSTITUTES OF RESEARCH

Overview

This is an alternative program offering guidance and placement assistance to students seeking employment on completion of high school. These students are non-college-bound seniors from the five inner-city high schools. The program emphasizes:

1. Guiding students to make decisions about their career goals
2. Assisting students to develop and maintain basic skills needed for their career choices
3. Finding jobs for all graduates at the job-entry level

Goals and Objectives

The overall goal is to assist inner-city high school students in finding gainful, full-time employment after graduation. The program provides:

1. Job development and placement services
2. Instruction in seeking and getting a job
3. Orientation to the world of work
4. Vocational counseling
5. Referral to educational and training opportunities
6. Interviews with businesses

   Counselors help students become:

1. Less fearful in job interviews
2. More aware of their own strengths and weaknesses
3. More informed on job-seeking techniques
4. More knowledgeable about the obligations and responsibilities of employment
5. Better acquainted with the world of work
6. More positive in attitude toward employment

Procedures, Methodology

The Job Development Program employs five fully credentialed counselors. These full-time counselors spend 35% of their time in individual counseling; group counseling takes up about 12% of their time. An additional 35% of their time is devoted to such tasks as consulting with other educational personnel, serving in community liaison roles, planning and evaluating program activities, and administrative duties. The remaining 20% of the counselors' time is devoted to identifying students' eligibility for job placement.

Five paraprofessionals are also employed. Approximately half of their time is spent in community liaison roles and another large part in working directly with students.

Facilities and materials are located in each of the five high schools and at the Board of Education building. These locations are known as the "Job Placement Center."

Evaluation

Evaluation data collection has focused on the number of students placed.

Placement over the past 6 years has been in clerical occupations, service occupations, skilled and manual occupations, and sales occupations. Only 18% of the graduating seniors placed 6 years ago were no longer employed. Ninety-five percent of the June 1972 graduates participating in the program were placed.

Contact:

Dr. Donald Healas
Director
Technical-Vocational Division
Cleveland Public Schools
1380 East Sixth Street
Cleveland, Ohio 44114

ANNOTATED LIST OF STRATEGY SOURCES

The following are listings of materials or activities for potential career guidance strategies.

1. *Resource book of low cost materials.* American Institutes for Research, 1974. P. O. Box 1113, Palo Alto, Ca. 94302.

A review of teacher handbooks and guides; career exploration, curricula, and student texts; student guidance materials; and multimedia resources. Also includes annotations of other bibliographies, journals, etc.; a survey of children's literature on career education; and brief notes of recently funded federal projects.

2. *Resource book of sample units.* American Institutes for Research, 1974. P. O. Box 1113, Palo Alto, Ca. 94302.

This resource contains 15 lesson units that teachers might use in the introduction of career education into their classrooms. The units cover grades K–9 and are intended to serve as examples of units teachers might develop themselves.

3. *Review of career education in secondary education.* College Entrance Examination Board, 1973. 888 Seventh Avenue, New York, N.Y. 10019.

A systematic review of development in secondary guidance in career education. This volume contains a description of trends and of exemplary guidance materials, projects, and programs now in use or development.

4. *Career guidance: A handbook of methods.* Merrill Publishing Company, 1973. Columbus, Ohio 43216.

5. *Career education resource guide.* General Learning Corporation, 1972. 2450 Embarcadero Road, Palo Alto, Ca. 94305.

This guide is not intended to be a comprehensive career education program. It is a collection of activities that can be initiated and carried out by teachers, K–adult. The activities are self-contained curriculum elements, selected and adapted as provocative classroom models. Materials and activities are organized according to performance objectives.

6. Gysbers, N., & Moore, E. (Eds.), *Career guidance, counseling and placement elements of an illustrative program guide,* 1974. University of Missouri, Columbia, Missouri.

Chapter 3 lists career guidance goals, objectives, and strategies for achieving them by grade level. Appendix B presents sample guidance strategies for goals and objectives in each of four basic domains: Self Domain; Life Roles, Settings and Events Domain; Life Career Planning Domain; and Basic Studies and Occupational Preparation Domain.

7. *Case studies in practical career guidance.* American Institutes for Research, 1973. P.O. Box 1113, Palo Alto, Ca. 94302.

This is a series of 13 case studies which were written as part of USOE contract: *Practical Career Guidance, Counseling and Placement for the Noncollege-Bound Students.* Other products include a review of the literature and final report which outlines a planning-evaluation model for developing local career guidance programs. All these products can be obtained through ERIC. Their respective ERIC numbers are listed below.

Baltimore Placement and Follow-up Program
Baltimore City Public Schools
Baltimore, Maryland   (ED 076 927)

Career Development Center
Troy High School
Fullerton, California   (ED 076 928)

Career and Educational Planning Program
Pioneer Senior High School
San Jose, California   (ED 078 332)

Career Guidance Program
Hood River Valley High School
Hood River, Oregon   (ED 078 333)

Computerized Vocational Information System
Willowbrook High School
Villa Park, Illinois   (ED 078 334)

Coordinated Vocational and Academic Education
North Gwinnett High School
Suwanee, Georgia   (ED 078 335)

Developmental Career Guidance Project
Detroit Public Schools
Detroit, Michigan   (ED 078 336)

Employability Development Team
Cleveland Public Schools
Cleveland, Ohio   (ED 078 337)

Job Development Program
Cleveland Public Schools
Cleveland, Ohio   (ED 078 338)

Kimberly Guidance Program
Kimberly High School
Kimberly, Idaho   (ED 078 339)

Lenawee Vocational-Technical Center and Placement Program
Adrian, Michigan   (ED 078 340)

Occupational Learning Center
Syracuse City School District
Syracuse, New York   (ED 078 341)

Youth Career Action Program
San Jose Unified School District
San Jose, California   (ED 080 078)

Practical career guidance, counseling, and placement for the noncollege-bound student: A review of the literature (ED 080 919)

Planning, structuring, and evaluating practical career guidance for integration by noncollege-bound youth (final report) (ED 082 073)
8. Mitchell, A. M., & Johnson, C. D. *Therapeutic techniques; Working models for the helping professional.* California Personnel and Guidance Association, 1973. 632 E. Commonwealth Avenue, Fullerton, Ca. 92631.

This entire book of 16 chapters describes intervention techniques which can be thought of as broad counseling strategies for guidance purposes. Successful working models are described for helping individuals achieve a reasonably positive self-concept, a sense of agency, and decisionmaking abilities.

In addition, for those who want to do more in-depth reading related to the topics of this chapter, the following may prove useful:

1. Campbell, R. E., Walz, G. R., Miller, J. V., & Kriger, S. F. *Career guidance: A handbook of methods.* Columbus, Ohio: Charles E. Merrill Publishing Company, 1973.

Chapter #4. Types of Career Guidance Methods. This chapter lists eight types of career guidance methods and discusses factors affecting the selection of methods. The eight types are: (a) behavioral approaches, (b) computer-assisted counseling, (c) educational media, (d) group procedures, (e) information systems, (f) simulation gaming, (g) vocationally relevant curriculum, and (h) work experience programs.

Chapter #5. Designing Career Guidance Approaches. This chapter is written to provide a framework for translating the needs of students into guidance goals and for designing tailored career guidance approaches which can help implement these guidance goals. The chapter focuses on: (a) presenting specific successful guidance approaches; (b) helping the reader determine if the approach would meet student needs of his district; (c) providing basic principles which govern the use of the approach; (d) providing concrete steps needed to design, implement, evaluate, and revise an application of the approach.

Chapter #6. Guidelines for Career Guidance Program Development. This chapter deals with total guidance programs rather than individual career guidance methods. It includes discussion of the following concepts which are relevant to this module's topic: (a) specification of alternative strategies, (b) program mission and accountability, (c) procedural parsimony, and (d) maximizing resources.

2. Jones, G. B., Ganschow, L. H., Helliwell, C. B., Wolff, J. M., & Dayton, C. W. *A manual for developing career guidance programs.* Irvine, Ca.: Educational Properties, Inc., 1974.

This manual is designed to teach the skills of program development. Chapter Three, Structuring and Implementing Programs, has content relevant to selecting guidance strategies.

3. Herr, E. L., & Cramer, Stanley H. *Vocational guidance and career development in the schools: Toward a systems approach.* Palo Alto, Ca.: Houghton Mifflin, 1972.

Although the entire book is relevant to developing a comprehensive career guidance program, Chapter 9, Helping Strategies in Vocational Guidance, is of particular interest. The author divides strategies into individual, group, and environmental treatment. Each of these types of helping strategies is discussed in terms of their relevancy for career guidance in the schools.

4. Stufflebeam, D. L. et al. Phi Delta Kappa National Study Committee on Evaluation, *Educational evaluation and decision making.* Peacock, Itaska, Illinois; Phi Delta Kappa, 1971.

Chapter 3, Educational Decision Making; and Chapter 4, Criteria, are particularly relevant to selecting strategies. A technical, detailed, but useful discussion of the process of choosing and the criteria for choice is included. These chapters would be helpful to an advanced student looking for a much more intellectual discussion of the topics.

5. Miller, J. R. *Professional decision making.* New York: Praeger, 1970.

The subtitle of this book is "A Procedure for Evaluating Complex Alternatives." It is written for complex business decisions but has application to this topic. It is highly technical, of interest only to an advanced student.

6. Kelley, Marjorie L. *Planning and design: The consideration of alternatives, Module 2.* San Francisco, Ca.: Far West Laboratory for Educational Research and Development, 1971.

This is one in a sequence of modules written for the educational developer. It outlines a pattern of operation to follow when considering alternative ways of reaching educational objectives. Good examples are provided and practice exercises are given to apply the skills learned.

Chapter 5

SUMMARY AND CONCLUSION

We have covered a good deal of ground in this discussion. Perhaps a brief recap would be in order.

Chapter 1, "The Need for More Systematic Program Planning and Evaluation," began by surveying some of the pressing problems facing human services programs today. These include the funding crisis in social and educational institutions, the crisis counseling syndrome, and the demand for accountability, which is a source of bewilderment for human services personnel. All of these factors become serious problems for human services programs. While a variety of possible answers exists, one particularly hopeful resolution rests in a systematic planning and evaluation approach. AIR has been working over the past two years to develop a competency-based staff development program to provide those working in human services with the knowledge and skills needed to plan, develop, implement, and evaluate comprehensive programs of guidance, counseling, placement, and followthrough. This approach has a number of advantages and disadvantages, and is presently being researched to determine whether it will fulfill its promise.

Chapter 2, "An Approach to Effective Program Planning and Evaluation," detailed this planning and evaluation approach, particularly its planning phase. Conducting desired outcomes assessments, performing current status assessments, establishing program goals, and developing client performance objectives were all delved into in some depth. Examples of activities and products involved in each of these tasks were presented. The remaining activities in the overall model for program development were then briefly summarized. These include:

Selecting Alternative Program Strategies
Specifying Process Objectives
Developing Program Staff
Trying Out Activities and Monitoring Early Implementation Efforts
Conducting Summative Evaluations (Cost-Impact Studies)
Communicating Evaluation Results

Chapter 3, "Developing Staff Skills for this Planning-Evaluation Model and Process," described the program of staff development that has been developed at AIR to help those working in human services to acquire the knowledge and skills needed to carry out such program improvement. Included was a discussion of some of the philosophical underpinnings for such staff development. The chapter then detailed the nature and focus of the program, and related this to general counseling skills. The format of the modules was presented. Each module is structured around precise objectives and includes all the following: an introductory section that outlines the module and indicates how it fits into the overall model; a glossary; text; discussion questions; practice activities; a postassessment; a personal application activity; and an appendix containing possible additional readings, an optional simulation description, and a bibliography of additional resources related to the topic of that particular module. Finally, the outcomes to be achieved by all the modules were presented.

Chapter 4, "Using Competency-Based Client Strategies and Materials," surveyed some of the programs now existing and described how these could fit into treatment strategies designed around the planning and evaluation approach detailed above. The following programs were briefly described:

> The Life Career Development System
> Bread and Butterflies
> Career Education and Satellite Technology Demonstration, 1974
> Decisions and Outcomes, 1973
> Career Guidance, Counseling, and Placement Guide and Career Education Methods and Processes, 1974
> Baltimore Placement and Follow-up Program
> Job Development Program—Cleveland Public Schools

Finally, an annotated list of resources was presented, summarizing many additional wellsprings of information and ideas for client treatment strategies and materials useful with any well-planned and evaluated program.

One additional related AIR effort should be mentioned here. This is a catalog of competency-based staff development programs existing throughout the United States. As part of the project that developed the education program described in this document, a national search was conducted to learn what other approaches existed that would be useful in developing human services staff skills. While the results of this search were not overwhelming, 34 other programs were described, many statements of desirable competencies for those working in this field were abstracted, and a catalog summarizing this information was produced. This is a resource useful for anyone interested in furthering the knowledge and skills of those working in guidance, counseling, placement, and followthrough.

Let us close with a hopeful thought. The possibilities to which human services programs can look, given imaginative leadership and hard work, are boundless. The services they can provide are invaluable. At no time in the past have the challenges been greater or the potential more limitless. The approach described in this document represents one attempt to help meet those challenges and experience the fulfillment of that potential. To those interested, we offer it as a tool in that effort. If it can help even a few people engaged in the endeavor of improving human services, our work will be well rewarded.

REFERENCES

The work of generating both the planning-evaluation model and the staff development program discussed in this document has of course involved the use of innumerable sources of information and ideas. We included those that seemed particularly relevant to Chapter 4 with that chapter, because they related so closely to the topic discussed (using client materials and approaches). Here are listed additional sources we found particularly helpful for the other topics we have discussed. These sources are grouped into six areas:

1. Human Services Personnel Development
2. Career Development Theory
3. Desired Outcomes Assessment
4. Current Status Assessment
5. Establishing Program Goals
6. Specifying Learner Performance Objectives

HUMAN SERVICES PERSONNEL DEVELOPMENT

Brammer, L. M., & Springer, H. C. A radical change in counselor education and certification. *Personnel and Guidance Journal,* 1971, *49,* 803–808.

Campbell, R. E. Applications of the systems approach to career guidance programs. *Focus on Guidance,* 1972, *4,* 1–11.

Carkhuff, R. R. A nontraditional assessment of graduate education in the helping professions. *Counselor Education and Supervision,* 1968, *7,* 252–261.

Cash, W. L., Jr. Message to the association. *Counselor Education and Supervision,* 1972, *11,* 161.

Engelkes, J. R., & Roberts, R. B. Rehabilitation counselor's level of training and job performance. *Journal of Counseling Psychology,* 1970, *17,* 522–526.

Ganschow, L. H., Hamilton, J. A., Helliwell, C. B., Jones, G. B., & Tiedeman, D. V. *Practical career guidance, counseling, and placement for the noncollege-bound student: A review of the literature.* Palo Alto, Ca.: American Institutes for Research, 1973.

Horan, J. J. Behavioral goals in systematic counselor education. *Counselor Education and Supervision,* 1972, *11,* 162–170.

Island, D. An alternative for counselor education. *Personnel and Guidance Journal,* 1972, *50,* 762–766.

Joslin, T. C. Knowledge and counselor competence. *Personnel and Guidance Journal,* 1965, *43,* 790–795.

The Guidance and Counseling Task Force. *A plan for the improvement of guidance services in California.* Sacramento, Ca.: California State Department of Education, 1973.

CAREER DEVELOPMENT THEORY

If you would like to know more about counseling theory, try any one of the following basic references:

Beck, C. E. *Philosophical foundations of guidance.* Englewood Cliffs, N.J.: Prentice-Hall, 1963.

McGowan, J., & Schmidt, L. *Counseling: Readings in theory and practice.* New York: Holt, Rinehart & Winston, 1962.

Patterson, C. H. *Theories of counseling and psychotherapy* (2nd ed.) New York: Harper & Row, 1973.
Steffler, B. *Theories of counseling.* New York: McGraw-Hill, 1965.

For an overview of the various theories of career development or more information on the process of career choice, see the following:

Borow, H. *Career guidance for a new age.* Boston: Houghton Mifflin, 1973.
Crites, J. O. *Vocational psychology.* New York: McGraw-Hill, 1969.
Herr, E. L. *Vocational guidance and career development in the schools: Toward a systems approach.* Boston: Houghton Mifflin, 1972.
Osipow, S. H. *Theories of career development.* New York: Appleton-Century-Crofts, 1968.
Shaw, M. C. *The function of theory in guidance programs: Guidance Monograph Series I.* New York: Houghton Mifflin, 1968.
Super, D. E., & Bohn, M. J. *Occupational psychology.* Belmont, Ca.: Wadsworth Publishing Co., 1970.
Tolbert, E. L. *Counseling for career development.* Boston: Houghton Mifflin, 1974.
Walz, G. R., Smith, R. C., & Benjamin, L. (Eds.) *A comprehensive view of career development.* Washington, D.C.: American Personnel and Guidance Association, 1974.
Zaccaria, J. *Theories of occupational choice and vocational development: Guidance Monograph Series IV.* Boston: Houghton Mifflin, 1970.

These are good sources for more in-depth information on particular theories:

Duncan, O. D., Featherman, D. L., & Duncan, B. *Socioeconomic background and achievement.* New York: Seminar Press, 1972.
Ginzberg, E. Toward a theory of occupational choice: A restatement. *Vocational Guidance Quarterly,* 1972, *20*(3), 169–176.
Holland, J. L. *Making vocational choices: A theory of careers.* Englewood Cliffs, N.J.: Prentice-Hall, 1973.
Roe, A., & Siegelman, M. The origin of interests. *APGA Inquiry Studies, No. 1.* Washington, D.C.: American Personnel and Guidance Association, 1964.
Schultz, T. W. *The economic value of education.* New York: Columbia University Press, 1963.
Super, D. E. Vocational development theory: Persons, positions, and processes. *The Counseling Psychologist,* 1969, *1*, 2–9.

Tiedeman, D. V., & O'Hara, R. P. *Career development: Choice and adjustment.* New York: College Entrance Examination Board, 1963.

For more information on methods and approaches in career guidance, see the following:

Bottoms, G., & O'Kelley, G. L. Vocational education as a developmental process. *American Vocational Journal,* March 21–24, 1971.

Campbell, R. E., Walz, G. R., Miller, J. V., & Kriger, S. F. *Career guidance: A handbook of methods.* Columbus, Ohio: Charles E. Merrill, 1973.

Gysbers, N. C., Drier, H. N., & Moore, E. J. (Eds.) *Career guidance: Practice and perspectives.* Worthington, Ohio: Charles A. Jones, 1973.

Hansen, L. S. *Career guidance practices in school and community.* Washington, D.C.: National Vocational Guidance Association, 1970.

Hoyt, K. B., Pinson, W. M., Laramore, D., & Mangum, G. L. *Career education and the elementary school teacher.* Salt Lake City, Utah: Olympus Publishing Company, 1973.

Tuckman, B. W. An age-graded model for career development education. *Journal of Vocational Behavior,* 1974, *4,* 193–212.

Willingham, W. W., Ferrin, R. I., & Begle, E. P. *Career guidance in secondary education.* New York: College Entrance Examination Board, 1972.

And for general interest:

Panel on Youth of the President's Science Advisory Committee. *Youth transition to adulthood.* Washington, D.C.: Office of Science and Technology, Executive Office of the President, June 1973.

Terkel, S. *Working: People talk about what they do all day and how they feel about what they do.* New York: Pantheon, 1974.

DESIRED OUTCOMES ASSESSMENT

If you want more general information on assessment, check:

Borg, W., & Gall, M. *Educational research: An introduction* (2nd ed.) New York: David McKay, 1971.

Fitzgerald, P. Assessing the perceived educational needs of students. *Education,* 1972, *92*(3), 13–14.

Fox, D. J. *The research process in education.* New York: Holt, Rinehart, Winston, 1969.

Issac, S., & Michael, W. B. *Handbook in research and evaluation.* San Diego: Robert R. Knapp, Publisher, 1971.

Kaufman, R., & Harsh, J. *Determining educational needs: An overview.* Washington, D.C.: U.S. Office of Education, 1969. (ERIC Document Reproduction Service No. ED 039 631).

Popham, W. J. *Educational needs assessment in the cognitive, affective, and psychomotor domain.* Los Angeles: Center for the Study of Evaluation, University of California at Los Angeles, 1969.

Rummel, J. F. *An introduction to research procedures in education* (2nd ed) New York: Harper & Row, 1964.

Wardrop, J. *Towards a broader concept of educational assessment.* (ERIC Document Reproduction Service No. ED 060 062). Paper presented at the Second Annual Mardi Gras Symposium, "Education: Instruction, assessment, and accountability," New Orleans, Louisiana, 1972.

If you would like more information on particular assessment approaches, try the following:

Cramer, S. The opinion survey as a research technique. In *Research guidelines for high school counselors.* New York: College Entrance Examination Board, 1966.

Flanagan, J. C. The critical incident technique. *Psychological Bulletin,* 1954, *51,* 325–358.

Hansen, J. C., & Herr, E. L. The follow-up study. In *Research guidelines for high school counselors.* New York: College Entrance Examination Board, 1966.

Jacobs, J. R. Effective follow-up study procedures. *The Guidance Clinic,* October 1–3, 1970.

Jung, S. M. Evaluative uses of unconventional measurement techniques. *California Educational Research Journal,* 1971, *22,* 48–57.

Lee, D. L. *Needs assessment model for guidance in North Dakota.* Bismarck, N.D.: North Dakota Department of Public Instruction, Guidance and Counseling Section, 1973.

CURRENT STATUS ASSESSMENT

For additional general information on assessment, see the following:

Best, J. W. *Research in education.* Englewood Cliffs, N.J.: Prentice-Hall, 1970.

If you would like more information on particular assessment techniques, see the following:

Buchheimer, A., & Weiner, M. Studying student attitudes. In *Research guidelines for high school counselors.* New York: College Entrance Examination Board, 1966.

Smith, T., & Johnson, C. D. *The priority counseling survey, high school; Form B.* Los Angeles: Educators Assistance Institute, 1971.

The following focuses on use of items rather than construction, and it includes helpful examples of open-form questionnaires for administrators and community members.

Hoyt, K. B. *Career education: What it is and how to do it.* Salt Lake City, Utah: Olympus Publishing Company, 1972.

If you want to know more about the concept and measurement of career maturity/development, see the following:

Cramer, S. H., & Herr, E. L. *Vocational guidelines and career development in the school: Toward a systems approach.* Boston: Houghton Mifflin, 1972.

Super, D. E. Computers in support of vocational development and counseling. In H. Borow (Ed.), *Career guidance for a new age.* Boston: Houghton Mifflin, 1973.

If you would like information about new career guidance programs, see:

Hansen, L. S., & Borow, H. Toward effective practice: Emerging models and programs. In H. Borow (Ed.), *Career guidance for a new age.* Boston: Houghton Mifflin, 1973.

ESTABLISHING PROGRAM GOALS

While a great deal has been written about behavioral objectives, surprisingly little is easily available on the topic of establishing goals. James Popham and Eva Baker, teachers in the instructional objectives field, have published *Establishing Instructional Goals* (Englewood Cliffs, N.J.: Prentice-Hall, 1970), but it deals with objectives far more than goals. Robert Mager, another expert in developing objectives, also has written a book on goals, *Goal Analysis* (Belmont, Ca.: Fearon Publishers, 1972), which is somewhat more directed at goals, but still largely focuses on objectives. The works of Benjamin Bloom and others are helpful. They are taxonomies of educational objectives, one in the cognitive and one in the affective realm. They are referenced in the next section of this bibliography, as is the work Frank Wellman has produced on a similar taxonomy for guidance-related objectives.

General reference works may provide some assistance; for example, books such as Stephen Isaac's *Handbook in Research and Evaluation* (San Diego: Robert Knapp, 1971). Finally, the series of California monographs published by the California Personnel and Guidance Association often touches on goals. These six monographs are:

Krumboltz, J. D. *Stating the goals of counseling.* (No. 1, 1966).
O'Hare, R. W., & Lasser, B. *Evaluating pupil personnel programs.* (No. 2, 1971).
Sullivan, H. J., & O'Hare, R. W. (Eds.) *Accountability in pupil personnel services: A process guide for the development of objectives.* (No. 3, 1971).
Mitchell, A. M., & Saum, J. A. (Eds.) *A master plan for pupil services.* (No. 4, 1972).
Cunha, J., Laramore, D., Lowrey, B., Mitchell, A., Smith, T., & Woolley, D. (Eds.) *Career development: A California model for career guidance curriculum, k-adult.* (No. 5, 1972).
Keirsey, D., & Bates, M. *Result systems management: The human side of accountability.* (No. 6, 1972).

Monographs are available from California Personnel and Guidance Association, 654 East Commonwealth Avenue, Fullerton, California 92631.

SPECIFYING LEARNER PERFORMANCE OBJECTIVES

A very good overall text on the subject of writing learner performance objectives is:

Kibler, R. J., Baker, L. L., & Miles, D. T. (Eds.) *Behavioral objectives and instruction.* Boston: Allyn and Bacon, 1970.

For information on the types of objectives, try reading:

Bloom, B. S. (Ed.) *Taxonomy of educational objectives. Handbook I: The cognitive domain.* New York: Longmans, Green and Company, 1956.
Krathwohl, D. R., Bloom, B. S., & Masia, B. B. (Eds.) *Taxonomy of educational objectives. Handbook II: Affective domain.* New York: David McKay, 1964.
Popham, W. J. et al. *Instructional objectives: American Educational Research Association Monograph Series on Curriculum Evaluation.* Chicago: Rand McNally, 1969.

For discussions on the purpose of writing objectives and their correct form, see:

Krumboltz, J. D. *Stating the goals of counseling, Monograph No. 1.* Fullerton, Ca.: California Personnel and Guidance Association, 1966.
Lindvall, C. M. (Ed.) *Defining educational objectives: A report of the Regional Commission on Educational Coordination and the Learning Research and Development Center.* Pittsburgh: University of Pittsburgh Press, 1964.
Mager, R. F. *Preparing instructional objectives.* Palo Alto, Ca.: Fearon Publishers, 1962.

The following contain many examples of objectives:

Dunn, J. A. et al. *Career education: A curriculum design and instructional objectives catalog.* Palo Alto, Ca.: American Institutes for Research, 1974.

National Assessment of Education Progress. *Objectives for career and occupational development.* Denver: Author, 1971.

Wellman, F. E. A conceptual framework for the derivation of guidance objectives and outcome criteria: Preliminary statement. In J. Whiteley (Ed.) *Research in counseling.* Columbus, Ohio: Charles E. Merrill, 1967.

The references below have more general information, but they contain parts which are relevant to the writing of learner performance objectives.

Briggs, L. J. *Handbook of procedures for the design of instruction.* Pittsburgh: American Institutes for Research, 1970.

Crawford, J. (Ed.) *CORD national research training manual* (2nd ed.) Eugene, Ore.: Teaching Research Division, Oregon State System of Higher Education, 1972.

Far West Laboratory for Educational Research and Development. *The specification of expected outcomes.* San Francisco: Author, 1971.

Herr, E. L., & Cramer, S. H. *Vocational guidance and career development in the schools: Toward a systems approach.* Boston: Houghton Mifflin, 1972.

Jones, G. B., Wolff, J. M. et al. *Specifying product and process objectives, Module 2.* Palo Alto, Ca.: American Institutes for Research, 1973.

Popham, W., & Baker, E. L. *Systematic instruction.* Englewood Cliffs, N.J.: Prentice-Hall, 1970.

Shaw, M. C. *School guidance programs. Objectives, functions, evaluation, and change.* Boston: Houghton Mifflin, 1973.

.